What oth

The Journey

I hope Steve Laswell keeps writing. It is his calling … God inspired. His writing is from the heart of God and his words are clearly inspired. This is all for His glory which knows no limits or boundaries. Be bold; be strong, for the Lord your God is with you!

—Dr. Ron

Thanks for sharing your thoughts. I admire Steve Laswell's ability to apply the lessons of every day to the discipline of our spiritual lives.

—Gordon

As a new Christian your writing has really been helpful in my spiritual guidance. Thank you.

—Erica

I am amazed by how much Steve Laswell can get out of scripture passages and relate them to daily living.

—Danny

This week's Journey was so fitting for me … it was like Steve wrote this exactly for me right now. We have so much going on, trying to make so many decisions and I feel we have gotten in the habit of just trying to get everything done that needs to be done and forgetting to ask for help from our Father and allow Him to guide us … having *The Journey* reminds me to create … more 'time' for praising God and handing my worries to Him.

—Deidra

I was reminded of how simple it is to know God more deeply and how ready He is to impart love and wisdom to me. I'm wondering why it had never occurred to me before to write down those conversations betweeen God and me! Of course when God speaks I want to remember what He says and now I have a way of doing that! Thank you Steve, for sharing that idea, so simple and yet so life-changing!

—Adele

I've really enjoyed week 19. Although, I know my mind is still fighting a lot of it... my heart knows what needs to be done. Thanks for the guidance!

—Kelly

One of my best friends is suffering through an alcoholic (husband) relationship told me that your message in *The Journey* this week gave her the hope to go on with her husband. Does God deliver in so many ways?

—Lucy

What a beautiful message. Steve Laswell always says just the right thing at just the right time. I'm still thinking about last week's closing prayer, "More of You, less of me."

—Dot

The Journey

Steve Laswell

The Journey

personal notes from the Father

TATE PUBLISHING & Enterprises

Published by Tate Publishing & Enterprises, LLC
127 E. Trade Center Terrace | Mustang, Oklahoma 73064 USA
1.888.361.9473 | www.tatepublishing.com

Tate Publishing is committed to excellence in the publishing industry. The company reflects the philosophy established by the founders, based on Psalm 68:11,
"The Lord gave the word and great was the company of those who published it."

Book design copyright © 2010 by Tate Publishing, LLC. All rights reserved.
Cover design by Blake Brasor
Interior design by Stephanie Woloszyn

Published in the United States of America

ISBN: 978-1-61566-952-3
1. Religion / Christian Life / Spiritual Growth   2. Religion / Christianity / General
10.03.09

TABLE
of Contents

Preface

"What we call the process, God calls the journey."

—Oswald Chambers

What you hold in your hands started in December 2006. That was when I sent the following email to my family and some friends in my support system of encouragers.

Subject: Out on the water...

That's what Peter did, climbed out of the boat, and started walking towards Jesus on the water.

It FEELS a little like that just now as I considered putting you on this email and daring to attach an "act of obedience."

Attached you will find Week 1 of 52 writings (Lord willing)... complied under the heading "The Journey... Personal Notes from God."

The first is "Watching & Waiting."

Gentle, constructive criticism and feedback is welcome, as is an opt-out request. For some reason (beyond the fact your email was in our address book) I have selected your name.

For years there has been a desire... and some encouragement to do this or something. So, the waves are real, Jesus is real in His call, and I'm climbing out... in full view of you who are with me in the boat.

Thanks for being in my life, as you are.

Maybe He has been watching and waiting for me to do this for some time (read the first attached); maybe He will encourage you today.

By the way, this is "rough draft" level stuff... do you feel like a "lab rat," yet?

That first entry has become the first chapter of this effort titled: *The Journey: Personal Notes from the Father.* The water was supporting my feet as I began a year long walk.

Then, it happened, some of the people replied with comments like...

It is constantly amazing how God can "speak" to us...

Please remember to put on the full armor of God and to know where the battle is fought... in the mind and that we do not wrestle against flesh and blood, but against principalities, against powers, against the rulers of the darkness of this age, against spiritual host of wickedness in the heavenly places.

I hope you hear your teaching on this being refreshed within your spirit... and that you step out in "full faith" for the work ahead.

May you sense His peace even before you have had a chance to read this.

—Danny

I will look and wait weekly.

—Lucy

Thanks for including us. I enjoyed the conversational style of your writing. As I read it, I'm reminded of one of my favorite Scriptures (parapharsed)... Hearts of stone turned into hearts of flesh... so you will be My people and I will be your God. (Ez 36:26–28)

Thanks for this. I have someone whom I believe will be blessed by your words. I've sent it along to her.

—Daleen

I agree, Steve, keep writing, be encouraged, courageous, and bold! Write it down and submit it. It is your calling. It is God inspired. Your writing is from the heart of God and your words are clearly inspired. This is all for His glory which knows no limits or boundaries. Be bold, be strong, for the Lord your God is with you!

—Ron

Just read week 9 today… thank you. There's A LOT going on in my life right now and this 'note from God' just confirmed some things that He has been saying to me. I liked this paragraph: Responses vary but are NOT optional: (how true!) either we seek to quiet ourselves in order to hear His voice or we turn up the 'noise of living' in an effort to silence His loving call on our allegiance. "

That's the key: understanding that no matter what He calls me to, HE LOVES ME and wants what is BEST for me. I believe that with all my heart.

—Claudia

So, that "act of obedience" was fueled by weekly accountability and the encouragement of individuals in my life. Could that be a guiding principle or "formula for faithfulness" along our journey as believers? Does such a clarity of commitment combined with accountability and encouragement lead to "success"?

For one year week after week, I wrote out of my journey and my personal quiet time with the Father. Until on December 31, 2007 I sent the following cover email for the last chapter…

Happy New Year!

Years ago laundry detergent companies put premiums in their boxes of detergent. It was a "little something" extra for their customers and a marketing bit to keep the unsuspecting consumer buying until they got the full set.

This week is a "bonus" – at least in the sense that it is something in addition to what is expected or strictly due… Week 53 of 52…!

Attached is your glass tumbler…

So, I write this week with the hope of contributing to your journey, especially at this time of transition. Enjoy."

Thank you for your time, concern, and interest… for being there, I thank God for you.

Grace and peace,
—Steve

The list of subscribers group named "My friends on The Journey" grew from a handful to over 100 through the natural marketing of friends sharing with friends. And the "act of obedience" was completed ... almost.

Then the question, what do I do with the writings, entries, messages, and notes from Abba? Some six months later, July of 2008 things began to happen with "the manuscript." It was an exciting day when Tate Publishing provided feedback that indicated there was something to work with and they had an interest in moving the project forward.

That is the story behind the book you hold in your hands. It will be fun to watch how God choses to speak into the lives of people on The Journey.

Grace and peace,
Steve Laswell
August 30, 2009

Introduction

Some of my journey

On September 3, 1954 the last new episode of The Lone Ranger aired on radio after 2,956 episodes over a period of 21 years. The masked Texas Ranger in the American Old West gallops about righting injustice with the aid of his clever, Indian sidekick Tonto. Departing on his white horse Silver, the Ranger would famously say "Hi-yo, Silver, away!" as the horse galloped toward the setting sun.

But what matters most was what happened the next day. For September 4, 1954 was "labor day" for my mother and the day my journey on earth began. No doubt a beautiful child (there are pictures) my parents Jim and Vivian Laswell welcomed me into their lives.

Not only was there the blessing of loving parents, but my fresh start provided me a faith-based heritage. The people who had gone before me expressed their faith in Jesus as the Messiah and Savior of the world.

There is one picture I cherish and can see from where I sit at the keyboard now; a black-n-white of my dad holding me. Less than two years old, we are standing in a retail photography store in Independence, Kansas. But it is the back of the photograph that adds the "priceless" component. The scrawled message, written in pencil by my great-grandmother on my dad's side, reads:

James Laswell and son - there darling little Baby Boy - may the Good Lord reward him for his work's sake.

Grandma Norman—with love.

Yes, I am thankful for my Christian Heritage, given on both sides of my family. My parents provided me opportunity to hear the Gospel from the start of my journey. In those days, it was common practice to have "revival" meetings at least once a year, often spring and fall.

One year, Rev. Johnny Whistler, a blind traveling evangelist came to the Church of the Nazarene in Neodesha, Kansas. Offerings to support Brother Whistler were a bit different when he came to town; he had a seeing-eye dog. Part of the "love offering" included cans of dog food, as well as the cash offerings.

The meetings were usually nightly, ending on Sunday. As a young boy in the second or third grade, I remember making my way to an altar of prayer to "accept Jesus into my heart, asking Him to forgive my sins and to be my Savior."

Just as soon as it was considered appropriate, around age 12, I was baptized as a follower of Jesus in the new church's baptistry. By God's grace, the gift of a hunger for Him was given me.

The journey of the journal

As a teen growing up in the church it was made clear to me the key to the Christian life is to read your Bible and pray. *But how was I to do this?* That remained a bit of a mystery.

Yes, I had my family, Sunday School, youth group, and devotional books but there was a longing for something more and a method to be consistent in my "devotions." It was my hunger for God that pushed me to seek Him in an effort to be like Jesus.

During my high school years I began to write some thoughts and prayers and Scriptures in a spiral notebook. I still have one of the early notebooks dated 1972. Who knew that it would be the beginning of a lifetime pursuit and practice?

Over the years, my quest for a consistent, relationship-building devotional life has matured into an effective spiritual discipline. The process is a systematic, effective, and powerful method used on a near daily basis for my personal quiet time of reflection and prayer.

What was my goal? To be a faithful follower of Jesus and have His help on the journey!

Fast-forward twenty years and I married Rita Van Dyne. With her support, I served as an Associate Pastor of Youth and Music in Baton Rouge; returned to the university to complete my undergraduate education. From there I received a call to my first "senior pastor" assignment, was ordained as an elder in the Church of the Nazarene, and finished my Master's of Ministry at Southern Nazarene University. We were blessed with three beautiful daughters.

Over the years I continued to cultivate the habit and practice of writing in my journal as a regular part of my personal quiet time with God. During the summer of 1992 Rita returned from a women's leadership conference. Through one of the speakers, the Lord spoke to her regarding the need to help our girls learn how to have their own personal quiet time, not just urge them to have their "devotions."

That particular summer day, Rita said, *"I've watched you over the years have your personal quiet time. How do you do it?"* The Holy Spirit spoke to me through Rita's question; was this something a spiritual leader would want to do for his wife and family?

Prompted by Rita's question I began to teach her, then a small group of other belivers how to use a journal for a more effective prayer life. That lead to the launch of *Battle Plan for Believers,* a non-profit ministry. It is my conviction that *Battle Plan for Believers* was raised up to serve others who want a growing relationship with God; to help people who want to learn how to journal and listen for Abba to speak in the place of prayer. As a result we developed a resource titled: *The Journey–A Personal Journal* and continue to find ways to equip believers who want to develop and enjoy more effective prayer lives.

The journey with your journal

Using the BPB personal journal, *The Journey* has helped believers from all walks of life. Jesus made it clear in His journey that the purpose of a consistent connection with God (through prayer) is to know Him, build the relationship, and thus be transformed into the likeness of Christ.

That is what I call *The Journey*. It was Oswald Chambers who correctly observed when he wrote: *"What we call the process, God calls the journey."*

When it comes to journal writing, I believe:

- It takes commitment, as a disciple of Jesus Christ, to use this simple, but powerful discipline

- Something significant happens to the experience and quality of the prayer time, when people use our unique method of writing in color

- The Holy Spirit brings life to your life through His Word and this spiritual discipline, when you are committed to developing a heart after God.

The Journey–A Personal Journal combines journaling with a Prayer Guide to provide a record of your spiritual pilgrimage. As the years pass, you will be amazed as you return to your Personal Journal. You will be able to remember God's faithfulness and see the transformation of your life into the likeness of Jesus.

The *Battle Plan for Believers* personal journal will help you develop and enjoy a growing personal relationship with God. The call of God on our lives is to walk daily, allowing the life of Jesus to be manifest through our lives.

The BPB Journal will allow you to:

- Record your spiritual journey

- Capture what God teaches you

- Reflect on your life in the pursuit of Christlikeness

- Record how God responds to your requests

- Manage your intercessory prayer ministry

Three voices, three pens

The truly unique concept applied to journal writing for spiritual growth is our use of three pens to represent the three voices found in communication with the Triune Godhead.

It really is quite simple and only requires a little faith to begin.

Black–*your voice to you;* this is the historical entry and answers the question regarding what is going on in your world at the time; context, it answers the question: what's been happening lately?

Green–*your voice to God;* you release thanksgiving and praise, ask questions, share your frustrations, disappointments, fears, hopes, dreams, and your thoughts to God.

Red–*God's voice to you;* this is God, your Father speaking in the *first person to you his child* in answer to the question: "Father, what would you like to say to me today?"

What happens when you adopt the three pens/three voices approach?

- It helps with the problem of distractions during your prayer time

- It brings focus to your conversation with Abba and sets up an expectation of two-way communication

- It allows you to see at a glance if you are doing all the talking or if you are listening; my definition of prayer is: *to listen much and speak also*

- It makes it easy to locate a specific thought you believe God has shared with you

Some would ask me, *"What about this writing in red? Aren't you afraid people will write something God didn't say?"* My response is summarized here:

- This works for people who have and want to cultivate a heart after God

- This works for people who desire to know God

- This works for people who want to be transformed into the likeness of Christ

- Truth is truth; all truth is God's Truth and ultimately found in His Word, therefore,

- If it violates Scripture it is not from God, no matter what color you write or language you speak

- This works for people who love God and want more of Him

- This works for people totally surrendered to Him

- Scripture teaches us to trust the Holy Spirit, our Teacher and Guide, while we are connected to a Community of Faith for protection from error

- There is always risk, but benefits exceed the risk

- This works for those with a faith-based love and hunger for relationship with God, not an agneda to push

Connecting this book with your journal

In the Preface you can read how this book came to be.

The question is: *How will you use The Journey: Personal Notes from the Father?*

- As a weekly guide to your daily personal quiet time appointment with God

- There is a weekly theme, Scripture references, introduction from me, and the potential living word from the Father to you; just show up and see what happens

- Explore the key words, Scriptures, and ideas in the text; ASK questions. Journal your thoughts, questions, and seek His input by asking *"What would you like to say to me this morning?"*

- Notice how thoughts and ideas show up at a specific time in your journey; listen

- It could be a fun way for your small group to journey together

Week 1

WATCHING AND WAITING

(First Sunday in Advent)

Devotional Scriptures

Luke 1:67–80
Colossians 1:9–23
Mark 1:1–8
Isaiah 43:1–13
Hebrews 10:11–25

The Psalmist's Pen

Psalm 97

FROM STEVE'S HEART

Does waiting come easy to you?

If you're like most people, waiting is a very difficult process. We hate long lines, we despise waiting lists, we're impatient at restaurants, and we must have the latest gadget as soon as it hits the market. If we have extra time, we might find great pleasure in going to a *waiting room* unless we forget to bring a book to read. But, at the mention of *waiting room,* most of us can relate the story of an unpleasant life experience.

Whether or not we enjoy the season of waiting, waiting in expectation is a vital part of The Journey. It is part of the faith adventure when we're *going without knowing* like Abraham of old (Hebrews 11). For me personally, there are several things I'm waiting for in expectancy this year—from jobs, to family circumstances, to relationships with friends.

Part of The Journey is about this watching and waiting, maintaining a spirit of expectation no matter what. In fact, waiting was necessary during the first Advent, when people were looking forward expectantly for the coming of the Messiah. Today, we are called to wait once again to stand on Jesus' promise that He will come again. We remind ourselves of the past while we wait and build our spirit of expectancy.

And by the way, we're not the only ones waiting in this human drama. The God who loved the world so much that He sent His one and only Son waits too.

FROM THE FATHER'S HEART

Since the beginning of time, waiting and watching have been a part of creation. With the coming of Advent, the world is reminded once again that waiting and watching are The Journey.

From "Day One" to "Day Two," through those first seven days of creation, I created and waited, created and waited. On "Day Six" I created man in My own image. I blessed them and encouraged them to enjoy. I waited and watched … until it happened—the first human fall came.

Next, I called out a people, my chosen people. The hand-me-down original failure from Adam and Eve created another dynamic to be dealt with. But I set a way of restoration into place for the damaged relationship.

For some four thousand years I worked with humanity, revealing Myself through Nature and My Divine Law written on man's conscience and on tablets of stone. Throughout history, I waited and watched for a response.

And so, "in the fullness of time," My waiting and watching culminated in the coming of My Son. Christ, the Word made flesh, appeared. Having given My Living Word, I began to write My ways on the heart of man. I now wait for man to respond to My gift of salvation.

So you see, waiting and watching is a principle of life, of creation for both of us. It is the stuff of relationships—it is life. The waiting process is present in seasons, in nature, and in life itself—conception, birth, development, growth, the seasons of human existence, the stages of life.

For just as surely as those of an earlier time longed for the Messiah, so I have spoken and it will be: His second visit.

And by the way, there is one more revelation: your life as one of My people.

Your life is to become a letter from Christ written not with ink but with My Spirit on your human heart. I want the life of Jesus to be revealed in your mortal body so those who are watching and waiting can see Me in you.

So you see, I am waiting and watching … still!

Don't lose heart; on the outside it may look like things are falling apart, but on the inside I am making new life. Not a day goes by without My provision and unfolding grace. Your hard times are nothing compared to the coming good times. I have an incredible celebration prepared. Things you see now are here today, gone tomorrow. Remember, the things you can't see now will last forever.

So don't fix your eyes on what is seen, but on what is unseen … watching and waiting. Waiting and watching; it has been that way since the beginning … for Me, too.

I am watching. I am waiting. Will you watch and wait with Me?

> I love you,
> Abba

YOUR HEART

In your quiet time with God, ask Him this question: "Father, what would You like to say to me today?" Write what you believe He is saying to you. Write your name, and begin to capture whatever comes to mind, just as if God were speaking to you. For you see, He is ...

Now, take a moment to write your thoughts to our Father.

Here are a couple of questions to help you reflect on watching and waiting:

- What is most encouraging to you from reading this week's thoughts?

- How do you keep from losing heart while watching and waiting?

Prayer

Father, thank You for sitting in the waiting room with me. Please help me to place my total confidence in You when I'm called upon to wait. Help me be still and know that You are God—faithful, merciful, trustworthy, just, and righteous in all Your ways. Grant me grace to maintain a vibrant spirit of expectancy based upon who You are and Your promises, not the circumstances and chatter of this world. In Jesus' name, amen.

ANTICIPATION

(Second Sunday in Advent)

Devotional Scriptures

Luke 1:57–80
Matthew 3:1–12
Luke 12:35–48

The Psalmist's Pen

Psalm 62

FROM STEVE'S HEART

My best friend is my wife, Rita. For over thirty-three years we have been on The Journey together and God has blessed us with three amazing daughters, three pretty cool sons-in-law, and eight grand-children. What can I say?

Saturday morning Rita asked, "Are you ready to get ready to go to Oklahoma City?" I was not quick to respond. She pressed on. "Your children are excited you are coming today." We were sitting on the sofa having coffee, looking out the window on a cold winter morning. Both of us were weary from a long week. I was emotion-ally drained from a few significant hits at work and exhausted from the endless list of house repairs. We were in the middle of remodel-ing our "new" twenty-five-year-old house—a project that was con-suming massive amounts of thought and energy. I had to admit I wasn't ready. I needed to *get ready* so I could be ready.

Readiness is about that point in time in which we are all set to move, to change course, to step out and act. But readiness does not come without disciplined preparation. In order for us to be prepared for the next movement in life, we have to get ready to be ready.

As a participant in a home remodeling project, I've learned a lot about tearing down, building up, and moving objects from one room to another to make things beautiful. In the process of updating our house, I've had to patiently wait and watch as our "new" home was getting ready.

The last big project is now our den downstairs, a task involving significant preparation. Before we can paint and redecorate the room, we must first relocate furniture, cover the floors, and sand down the walls. It's a long process, and discipline is necessary. Once the carpets are protected and the walls prepped, we will be ready for the fun part of painting. Although these long hours of "getting ready to be ready" may seem extraneous, they are required for the end result—a beautiful new den for our family.

Just like remodeling a home, there are times in life when we are getting ready, so we'll be ready for whatever is next. Whether a job changes, a new direction in ministry, a shift in the family, or a new season in life we have to be faithful and get ready. As we discipline ourselves in preparation, we'll be able to continue the journey with God into the spacious place He has for us. Are you ready or do you need to get ready?

FROM THE FATHER'S HEART

Getting ready is disciplined living which allows you to *be ready*. When you are in the habit of getting ready you will be ready. This will allow you to enjoy the celebration of life's moments and your ministry assignments. Getting ready requires watchfulness, which is part of the calling on your life as My child. It means you are living life observantly, vigilantly, and alertly. Most people just stumble along The Journey.

Being watchful is to look in two directions. The first is to look and wait expectantly for the return of Jesus, as men waiting for their master to return. The second is to look at yourself and your place in life and wait expectantly. When My Son Jesus returns, I want to find you faithful doing the work I have called you to do.

To live *looking expectantly* is to live as if My Son Jesus may show up at an hour when you are not expecting Him. To live watchfully impacts the choices of your day. This outlook becomes a means of grace.

Look at the life of Zechariah, the father of John the Baptist. He was on duty and serving as a priest before Me. He was chosen and faithful in his calling, but he was not living expectantly. When My angel told him he and his wife were to have a son who would be mightily used by Me, he was caught off guard. When the moment came, it lost some of its glory because Zechariah was not ready. However, My purpose was not hindered. Be encouraged while challenged with this reality. Getting ready is to *be* ready. As you wait and watch in obedience, you will not only be ready for My appearance, but you will also share My joy in that moment.

My appearance to you is, of course, the second visit of My Son, Jesus Christ the Lord. But My appearance also relates to Jesus showing up today in your life path along The Journey. If you're ready for My Son, you will recognize Him as you minister to those around you in your daily life. You will recognize Him when your mate needs an encouraging word or assurance of your love, respect, and loyalty. You will recognize Him when a little one in your life requires an example or when he may need affection, training, or correction. You will recognize Him when a co-worker or a friend needs a smile and a kind word. You will recognize Him when you find others who are searching for life and need you to share The Answer.

Eternity invades the common ground of today when you are waiting, watching, and getting ready. When you live ready, a moment will come find you, and I will be there. Once you are dressed ready for service you will serve. As you live getting ready, you will be ready.

Your approach to life will be marked with a faith-based expectancy, and the glory of the moment will not be lost on you.

Remember, the simplest gesture offered in the "Spirit of Jesus" honors Me. A warm smile … an encouraging word … bending down to the eye level of a little one … speaking kindly to senior adult as she sits having lunch by herself … Even the simplest act of ministry can be marked by the joy that comes from being ready and available.

I want you to rethink what it means for My Son Jesus Christ to come. In so doing, you will reap the grace-gift of living life in the present moment. You will make healthy choices for all your relationships. Your daily walk will be filled with My presence. As you partner with Me in touching the lives of others, you will experience great delight and joy.

Along your journey, you will need rest. Waiting, watching, and remaining ready can wear you out. Just remember to come to Me often for your rest. Come into My presence knowing that your hope, your security, and your salvation are all in Me. When you rest in Me, the Rock of your salvation, there is no need to be shaken. Your honor depends on Me; simply allow Me to be your Mighty Rock and Refuge. Before your day begins and at the end, come to Me and find rest.

Getting ready is a disciplined part of living the life as a follower of Jesus. It makes The Journey an *adventure*. A ready response allows you to enjoy the celebration of the moment—a moment of ministry shared with My Son, Jesus.

I love you,
Abba

YOUR HEART

In your quiet time with God, ask Him this question: "Father, what would You like to say to me today?" Write what you believe He is saying to you. Write your name, and begin to capture whatever

comes to mind, just as if God were speaking to you. For you see, He is ...

Now, take a moment to write your thoughts to our Father.

Allow these questions to help you define your state of readiness:

- What would you need to change to live in constant watchfulness and alertness?

- How will you be aware of needs around you? Are you willing to serve others even if it's inconvenient?

- What has Jesus called you to do?

- How can you live each day with an expectancy of His return?

- What areas of discipline do you want to improve in?

- What would it take for you to rest in the Father's care?

Prayer

Our Father, thank You for the call to "get ready". Grant me grace to live a disciplined life of getting ready so that I will be ready for Jesus' return but also for the assignment You have for me today. I want to be prepared for the people You send across my path. Let me offer the Ministry of Jesus and glorify Your Name. Amen.

Week 3

TAPPING YOUR RESOURCES

(Third Sunday in Advent)

Devotional Scriptures

Mark 13:1–13
Revelations 1:1–8
John 1:14–18
Ezekiel 34:11–16
Acts 1:1–11

The Psalmist's Pen

Psalm 80

FROM STEVE'S HEART

A couple of years ago, several thoughts began to emerge from my journey. As a result, I developed a list called *Current Top Ten Influential Practices*, which presents my guiding thoughts towards life lived out in the work place and on The Journey itself. The foundational presupposition of these practices is living to please God every day.

Steve's Current Top Ten Influential Practices

1. Live by priorities—God, family, work, today list

2. Care … but not too much

3. Fill other's buckets

4. Ask more, tell less

5. Delegate at 80%

6. Think—what am I thinking?

7. More face-to-face, less electronic

8. Tap into my resources

9. Read, read, read

10. Exercise more, eat less

As I was focusing on number 8, I began to take note of my resources. Resources are natural features or talents that enhance the quality of one's life. If you're reading this you have many resources available to help you succeed in life, too.

Part of my list includes my heritage and family members, my education and life experiences, my talents and skills, my mentors and people along my journey, my network of people, my personality as well as my outlook, my faith-based worldview and personal relationship with God.

Indeed, my resources are not restricted to the natural realm. A resource can also be a source of information or expertise. Who better than God is there for us to turn to for help living life well? Our Father has a myriad of resources available for me, for us every day. Because these resources flow from God, they are perfect, infinite, and always accessible. The fact is that I will not complete The Journey to my full potential if I depend on natural resources alone; they are limited. To fulfill my purpose, I must rely on the resources of God.

Our Father is not calling us to walk this Journey spiritually *un*equipped. He offers major resources and is beckoning us to draw from Him, from His wisdom, strength, and power. We are invited to come to Him in true humility, realizing our own physical and intellectual resources are not enough for The Journey. As we accept His grace for The Journey, we will find ourselves being transformed into kingdom representatives and walking at our full potential.

From the Father's Heart

My dear child, it grieves Me to watch you struggle when I am available as one of your resources for The Journey. Have you ever noticed what happens to you when you don't use Me as your primary resource? Your stress goes up while your joy fades; your anxiety rises and your peace erodes; your emotional reactions kick in as your Jesus-like response slips away.

I want you to know that I am here for you. Please tap into Me and all that I offer. My grace, My wisdom, power, and love are available to you as your ultimate resource for The Journey.

The secret to tapping into My resources is *humility*. Humility allows you to *not* experience shame, hesitance, or resistance in expressing your need of Me. The Psalmist, Asaph, recognized the desperate need for Me in his life and generation as he cried out, "Restore us … make your face shine on us. Restore us, O Lord God Almighty; make your face shine upon us, that we may be saved."

To approach Me in humility is to come before Me without any shame even though your life is in a mess due to destructive, self-defeating self-rule. Humility frees you to declare your need of My help, My gift of salvation, and My restoration. True humility allows you to reach out and receive My grace.

Don't let pride prevent you from receiving Me. Pride is the self-deceived state of those who say, "All is well! I've got it together. I am ruler and god of my own life. My destiny is in my hands." A humble heart is one that will honestly acknowledge reality. If you're walking in humility, you will understand that you can't do it all on your own.

In your time of darkness and helplessness, if you come to Me, I have good news for you. By definition, *good news* is delivered in the context of a bad situation. So when your life includes confusion, disappointments, or sorrow come to Me. I have good news for you!

There have been many people in history who were bearers of good news. John the Baptist, for instance, was a deliverer of the good news of coming salvation. He was chosen by Me to tell the world that My Son had come. John, the Disciple of Jesus, was also a carrier of good news. In his writing, he reminds you of the true reality: Jesus is the Alpha and the Omega, the beginning and the ending…which is, and was, and which is to come, the Almighty.

So, My child, I want you to draw close to Me in humility, opening your ear to hear My good news. Allow Me to be your primary resource for The Journey. Don't assume you can handle life alone; realize you need My grace daily. As you begin to come near to Me in humility and expectancy of heart, I will speak to you of My goodness and My salvation. I will give you My resources for your journey and to extend to those around you. How would you like to spread Good News?

I love you,
Abba

YOUR HEART

In your quiet time with God, ask Him this question: "Father, what would You like to say to me today?" Write what you believe He is saying to you. Write your name, and begin to capture whatever comes to mind, just as if God were speaking to you. For you see, He is…

Now, take a moment to write your thoughts to our Father.

Take time to create your list of resources using these questions to guide your reflection:

- What does it mean for you to tap into your resources?

- What resource have you overlooked that, if you tapped into it, might help you through this season of your journey?

- How might you offer your resources to others to help them along their journey?

- What are your hobbies and skills, and how can you use these to serve others?

- What resources are available to me as a child of God?

- How can you tell someone about the good news of salvation?

Prayer

Father, Thank You for Your resources; Your wisdom, grace, strength, and willingness to help me. Grant me grace to live in humility so I will recognize my need for You, just for today. Forgive me for those times when I think I can handle life alone and fail to consult You. Help me tap into Your love for me and all that You offer me for the Journey. Thank You for Your Word, the Good News of Your plan for my life. Use me today and open a door so I may share the Good News with others who need to know You. Amen.

Week 4

TOGETHER

(Fourth Sunday in Advent)

Devotional Scriptures

James 5:7–18
Matthew 1:18–25
Isaiah 7:14; 9:1–7; 40:1–11;
John 1:1–19
Ezekiel 34:17–31

The Psalmist's Pen

Psalm 65

FROM STEVE'S HEART

As I have noted, Rita and I have been married for over thirty-three years. Not only is she my best friend and helpmate, she is also my partner on The Journey. She means so much to me, and I enjoy walking through our journey together. Just this morning, I told the Father, "My love and appreciation of Rita grow the longer we travel this journey together. What a wonderful woman, lovely lady, magnificent mother, wife, and helpmate. Thank you so much for this gift. What a crown on my head she is!"

The two of us are experiencing a great season in life. Since our kids are on their own, we have more time to enjoy each other and our present assignments in life. Each season has responsibilities that are to be embraced and enjoyed. We enjoy our morning coffee quiet time and chats, walking together, and those leisurely conversations after dinner. We've enjoyed trips, whether to Top Sail Island or Branson; time away, just the two of us.

Being empty nesters also has the added benefit of a quiet and peaceful house. We shut off the upstairs now; for the most part, house cleanings last longer and the kitchen ... well, that is really different, from meal preparation to keeping the dishes done. Did I mention the ability to sit still? Whether reading, or outside by our Kio pond, or with that cup of coffee, it's amazing how quickly one can grow accustomed to quiet.

Around Christmas time, however, all that quietness is exchanged for loud voices and running feet as our grandkids and their parents come home for Christmas. Our two-person residence is now overflowing with more than a dozen family members. Did I mention that six of them are under the age of six?

The amount of stuff hauled in for a brief visit is amazing! Extra booster seats, electronic gadgets for surveillance, child raising products we never heard of. The extra "helping hands" in the kitchen (Grandma is so patient). The upstairs playroom is carpeted with toys and books pulled off the shelves; the character building work of sharing is heard with *occasional* outbursts of vocalized complaints. The questions regarding snacks or when we're going to eat (often within an hour or two of just putting the kitchen back in order) are consistently raised.

Bath time and bedtime are quite different from the norm. Our married kids staked out their bedrooms from the first visit. Story time can be "read it again" to "sing it again" until finally I muster up the courage to say it is time to pray. It depends on who has started praying out loud at home as to which grandchild volunteers to pray or sing the prayer they know. The sleeping bags, extra pillows, and individually selected stuffed animals are claimed for the long trip from tucking in to falling asleep and, "No, you can't have another drink until morning."

Our lives and home totally transform when our children and

grandchildren visit. The steady pace of life zooms to warp speed, and the quiet days are filled with laughter, high levels of activity, and chaos. All personal space is obliterated as loved ones fill every room. The moment our family steps into our house, everything is changed.

Having my family home for Christmas reminds me of the change that occurs anytime others come into our lives. For example, when a man and woman come into each other's lives through marriage, two separate individuals are melded into one covenant union. When a couple has their first baby, their identity transforms from "husband and wife" to "family." With each additional child added to the family unit, the dynamic continues to grow and change. Every time a person comes into our world, our life will never be the same.

The word *come* means to move into view, to happen in time; to be available; to arrive at a specific point as a consequence of orderly progression; to proceed toward a specific place. The coming of another not only brings change, but it also brings progress. It propels us to a certain destination, and always brings us closer to the ones who come to us.

Our relationship with God is a continual journey of *coming*. Throughout history, God has always made steps to come closer to humanity. His Spirit is ever pursuing the hearts of men, and His desire is to come close to each of us. Our responsibility is to respond to His coming.

Once He comes into our lives, we are never again the same. When God comes on the scene, everything changes—our circumstances, our attitudes, and hearts. As we allow Him to come into our daily routine, even our little moments are transformed. Every time He comes to us and we come to Him, something wonderful inevitably occurs.

The process of coming is not only about transformation; it is also about progression towards a destination. This coming keeps and guides us along The Journey, helping us reach the destiny our Father has for us. More importantly, this coming is a continual effort of the Father God to move us into a closer place with Him.

FROM THE FATHER'S HEART

I am pleased to see you enjoying our time together. It delights Me every time you welcome and connect with Me. You have no idea how My time with you transforms you into the likeness of Jesus.

Stuff happens when I come. Nothing is the same once My presence enters the picture. When I first came and spoke those creative words, there was chaos. The earth was formless and empty; darkness was over the surface of the deep. But I spoke creation into existence. Day and night; darkness and light; water and land; sky, sun, moon, and stars—these came into being as I spoke. I called forth the trees and the vegetation, the birds, the fish, and all the animals. I then created man, made in My image, to rule over everything that I had made. I am Creator God, and My spoken Word gets things done.

But Satan and sin destroyed My perfect creation. Humanity became broken and man needed restoration. So the moment in history arrived for My Word to come; it was time to redeem and restore.

This time My Word became flesh, taking on human form and walking on the earth. Jesus, the Word, offered the reality of life and the opportunity of restored relationship between us: judgment, forgiveness, hope, peace, joy, mercy, grace, freedom, victory, and love. My Son came to call things back into rightness, alignment, order, and restoration. Once again I came to the place of chaos, where darkness sought to snuff out the light, and I spoke life.

When I came to the world, some did not even notice. Some did not want Me to come as I came, and others did not want My Son, Jesus. But those who accepted the coming of My Son experienced a life-changing moment along The Journey. I am still the same today. When I come, I bring My creative Word to your life. I restore and recreate you, and bring you into My family.

I have come, and I am here. Will you receive Me? The Journey is about My coming and your receiving Me—season after season, year after year. It is a continual process of building your faith in Me and My Son for your salvation. When I come and you receive Me, stuff happens—salvation, restoration, and transformation into the likeness of Jesus.

All this builds on itself—layer upon layer, season after season, towards the maturity of a Spirit-directed daily life with better choices and responses. Transformation is made possible because I came. It is My delight to offer you My coming. As a result of our contact redemption, salvation, restoration, and transformation invades your whole experience in the world as a human being created for fellowship.

I am the God Who Comes. I came, moved into view, and arrived on time with an orderly progression since the Beginning. I continue to be approached as the God Who Comes, coming to you. Together, we proceed toward a future place that is just as real as where we've been in the past.

Today, when I come, I come to you as the Creator, Holy God, Messiah, Savior, and Redeemer. When I come, I come loving and caring, desiring a response—your response of love and commitment in return. Be still and know I am God. Be still and sit in amazement. I will come to where you are.

For all who wait, watch, and hope for Good News—there is still hope, for I am the God Who Comes. I came, I come, and I will come. Historically, it has been as Scripture reveals. There is a scheduled time in the future when My Son Jesus will come. And at that moment, every knee shall bow in heaven, on earth, and under the earth to the name of Jesus. Every tongue will confess that Jesus Christ is the Lord, to My glory as God the Father.

Recognize My mercy and grace, and continue to be drawn into the grand mystery of salvation. Know that I am continually coming to you and long for you to come to Me. Together, we are proceeding toward the wonderful future I have for you.

I love you,
Abba

YOUR HEART

In your quiet time with God, ask Him this question: "Father, what would You like to say to me today?" Write what you believe He is saying to you. Write your name, and begin to capture whatever comes to mind, just as if God were speaking to you. For you see, He is…

Now, take a moment to write your thoughts to our Father.

Take a moment to remember times when you were aware of God's coming to you and reflect on the following:

- What is most encouraging to you from reading this week's thoughts?

- What events brought you to the decision to receive Christ as your personal Savior? How did God "come" to you?

- What are you doing to respond to the Father's invitation to come to Him?

Prayer

Father, thank You for coming. Thank You for reaching out to Me in love and mercy when I was lost and didn't know You. Thank You for sending Your Son Jesus to restore me to a right relationship with You. I am so grateful to be a part of Your family! I make a decision today to continue to respond to Your coming. Help me to be sensitive to Your Spirit as You continue to draw me into You. Amen.

GIFT FROM GOD

(First Sunday After Christmas)

Devotional Scriptures

Exodus 19 & 20:18–26
1 Corinthians 10
Galatians 3:22–4:7
2 Corinthians 5:16–21
John 3:1–8
Ephesians 1:3–14

The Psalmist's Pen

Psalm 96

FROM STEVE'S HEART

Nolan, our three-year-old grandson, was so excited when he opened his hot red racecar, Lightening McQueen—a talking, programmable car of recent movie fame. We had to require him to set it aside so he would open his other Christmas gifts. But no other present compared to this fast, motorized toy... that is until his little brother Levi opened the big box—Disney's Tigger the Airplane. This preschool toy was complete with lights on the rotating propeller, more buttons to push—all with the appropriate sounds, of course—and the capacity for a child to sit on it flying through the room! Now that challenged little Nolan's young heart for the greatest gift.

Truth is Nolan will remember Lightening McQueen for only a

short period of time. First, I doubt the toy itself will last too long—as a three year old, Nolan is all-boy. But more importantly, his desire for a car will change and mature over his lifetime.

God's greatest gift is not about stuff, not even all the good stuff we often count as a "blessing" in life on this planet. As we mature in wisdom and discover the truth revealed in the Scriptures, we begin to realize what matters most. The Journey is a process of knowing God's Greatest Gift—Jesus.

The word *gift* means a notable capacity, talent, or endowment; something voluntarily transferred by one person to another without compensation. God's greatest gift comes from *His* capacity; all that is required is our willingness to receive what He voluntarily offers to transfer to us. Listen for Him to speak to you about His Greatest Gift...

FROM THE FATHER'S HEART

Imagine you had an unknown physical need—a *life-threatening* need. What if you did not know you had this life-threatening need, although it impacted your day-to-day life? How would you feel? Although you were unaware of its existence, this hidden condition was the root cause of a substandard and unhealthy life. Because it is a life-threatening situation, finding a cure to your problem would be your greatest need.

To press the point further, imagine your life was characterized by a state of under-performance—routinely missing the mark and habitually failing to live to your full potential. Finally, you discover what has been undermining your success. You connect the dots and discover your greatest need, this *life-threatening* need. How would you feel?

The law was the old covenant of rules and regulations given to guide man's interaction with Me, with life, and with others. The purpose of the law was to make obvious to everyone that you are, in yourself, out of right relationship with Me. That is a *life-threatening* situation now revealed.

Furthermore, the law showed the futility of devising some "religious system" for getting by on your own efforts. This great need created a condition impacting your very existence. To top it off, there is *nothing* you can do about it. How does *that* make you feel? Discouraged? Desperate? Hopeless?

When you realize your true situation without Me, you are ready to receive the answer, the solution, and the cure for your life-threatening need. You are ready to receive My greatest gift.

The moment in history arrived when I sent My Son Jesus. He was born among you of a woman. He was born under the conditions of the law so that He might redeem those who had been kidnapped by the law. These happened so you could be set free and enjoy your rightful existence; this was My fix for your greatest need. My greatest gift was given to address your greatest need—a restored relationship with Me, your Creator God.

Still, I come to wherever hope is absent, pain is plentiful, confusion is constant, brokenness is the norm, loneliness abounds, and rebellion is rampant. Wherever there is fear of failure, boredom, bitterness, lack of forgiveness, or the consequences of poor choices—I come there. My greatest gift is perfectly designed to meet your greatest need.

It saddens Me that many reject My gift. Some do not understand the freedom of what I offer. Because I am extending salvation without strings attached, some do not feel worthy of My gift. Others reject My gift because they think they don't have the faith to receive it. And some refuse My gift, because they do not want to acknowledge their need.

Sooner or later, everyone will have to face Me and appear before the judgment seat of Christ. At that great moment in history, every person will be judged for their actions during their life on the earth. Just as sure as you were born and are alive today, you will one day stand in the place of judgment. Once you accept this reality, you will begin to understand My greatest gift.

I love giving gifts to my creation. Your life is filled with gifts that have come from My heart—the beauty of nature, your health and intelligence, your talent and money, the love for your spouse and your family. Those are indeed gifts to be enjoyed and appreciated, along with My gifts of creativity, productivity, food, sight, hearing, and the amazingly complex human body. There are so many gifts that I give you every day that you take most of them for granted.

But the greatest gift I could ever offer you is the precious gift of salvation through My Son. Through this gift, I will not count your sins against you when you appear before the judgment seat of Christ. This gift of forgiveness, reconciliation, and righteousness is made possible through the cross. Jesus came and died so that you would no longer live for yourself, but live for Me.

The Journey is about learning, knowing, sharing, and living out salvation in your life. Once you experience My love and forgiveness, you learn to love and forgive yourself. Then, you become free to love and forgive others. You connect the dots and walk in freedom.

Long before I laid down earth's foundations, I had you in mind as the focus of My love—to be made *whole and holy* by My love. Long, long ago I decided to adopt you into My family—and by the way, I took great pleasure in planning this!

I want you to enter into the celebration of My lavish gift giving. Because of the sacrifice of the Messiah you're to be a free person——free of the penalties and punishments chalked up by all your misdeeds. This is My gift to you, which will allow you to stand before My Son when He comes to judge the world. My greatest gift is one you will never outgrow, outlive, or fully comprehend, no matter how long you live, until we're face-to-face.

I love you,
Abba

YOUR HEART

In your quiet time with God, ask Him this question: "Father, what would You like to say to me today?" Write what you believe He is saying to you. Write your name, and begin to capture whatever comes to mind, just as if God were speaking to you. For you see, He is...

Now, take a moment to write your thoughts to our Father.

Stop for a few moments to contemplate on God's greatest gift to you. Here are some questions to help you on your Journey:

- Do you remember a favorite present from your childhood? How did you feel when you opened it?

- When did you accept God's greatest gift? What stands out to you as you remember the day you placed your faith in Jesus as your personal Savior?

- How do you take God's daily gifts for granted? How might you change that?

- What can you do today to help pass on God's greatest gift to another person?

Prayer

Father, thank You for all Your gifts and help me live with a heart of gratitude. Most of all help me to recognize Your solution for every need I have along my journey—right now, where I am today. Grant me grace to welcome Your love, mercy, and forgiveness, and to receive You every day that I may walk in wisdom and be pleasing to You. Reveal Your solution for all of My relationships and choices along The Journey. Amen.

Week 6

GOD'S AMAZING CHOICE

Devotional Scriptures

John 15:12–17
Romans 5:6–11
1 Thessalonians 1:2–10
Isaiah 42:1–9
Luke 10:1–12
1 Peter 2:1–10
Colossians 3:12–17

The Psalmist's Pen

Psalm 89:1–18

FROM STEVE'S HEART

Do you remember those playground games that required the selection of teams? Whether it was at recess, in gym class, or for a neighborhood athletic event, the ritual of choosing teams was always a necessary rite of passage during our childhood.

The process of team selection usually began with the teacher or coach picking two stellar athletes. The team captains would then choose their players, calling out names one by one.

For those who were athletically gifted or skilled, this was a moment filled with anticipation. Would I be selected as captain this time? Will my name be called out in the first round of chosen teammates? But for those who lacked finesse or popularity, this was an incredibly awkward moment. *How far down the list will I be this time? Will I be the last name called?* As the process of elimination continued, confidence would shrivel and embarrassment would increase as the draft pool came down to the last two.

The pain of being last only increased when an odd number of kids showed up to play. The "odd man out" became the substitute sitting on the bench. The only recourse was to act like it didn't matter while sauntering off across the playground to do something else.

This ritual only worsened when there was an extra player on one team. The person whose name was called last was then designated as substitute player number one! The implied value needed no added words of explanation. There was nothing left to do but play like it didn't matter while trying to disappear into the excitement of the chosen ones ringing in our ears.

To be chosen is an inherent desire in each of us. In our hearts, we secretly long to be accepted, preferred, and counted worthy. We yearn to hear our names called, not because we were the last ones available, but because someone saw value in us. We all desire to be *chosen* by someone for something.

The word *chosen* actually means to select freely and after consideration; to decide on especially by vote; to have a preference for. From my experience with the voting process, I am extremely thankful God's choice of me is *not* based on some vote! Indeed, it is a testament to God's love and mercy that He selected us *freely* and *after consideration*. It is amazing that the Creator of all things has a *preference for me!* What a wonderful foundational reality to comprehend as we progress in our Journey. We are chosen by God!

FROM THE FATHER'S HEART

In the real "game" of eternity, things are quite different from the playground. You see, it's not a question about whether or not you will be chosen. As Jesus revealed, you did not choose Him, but

He chose you. You are already chosen. After great consideration, I selected you and waited. I continue to wait daily for your response. The question is how will you respond as I call your name?

People often think they bring a lot to the table. They think "*The team captain would be crazy not to want me on the team!*" Indeed, you may have the coveted skills and knowledge for a spelling bee, a math competition, the debate team, a vocal ensemble, two-on-two hoops, or a summertime softball game. But I did not choose you for your natural ability, your brains, your skill, or your popularity.

When I called your name, you were dead in your sinful, rebellious, no-time-for-God, self-centered, self-ruling life. You were a sinner. My love-based operation searched you out. You were selected because I have a preference for people who don't have it all together.

Yes, it remains a simple story: I loved you so much that I gave My Son to die for you. I did not want sin to destroy you. I did not want you to be left on the sidelines, rejected. I did not want you off alone, wondering how to live life. Through My Son, I presented a simple solution for you to have a whole and lasting life.

While everybody was standing around on the playground with nothing whatsoever to offer, My Son Jesus Christ arrived to make things happen. He presented Himself for that law-based, sacrificial death while you were too weak and rebellious to do anything to get yourself ready. I call your name so you can be set right with Me.

I have chosen you for Me. But I have also chosen you for obedience. I want you to obey My commands and remain in My love, just like Jesus did while alive on earth. I have chosen you to exemplify My love to the world.

As a chosen one, you are fashioned for a changed life. Once you became a follower of Jesus, you believed the Scripture revelation regarding what this game of life is about. The Journey is movement from death to life ... from bondage to freedom ... from self-destructive, self-government to abundant living with Jesus as Lord. As a chosen one, you are to begin living life in the pattern of Jesus.

Make no mistake; I am calling your name. I chose you to be on My team as My ambassador and representative. I chose you to experience life so that all your relationships will be enjoyed within the boundaries of love. I chose you to spread the Good News and to make a difference in a world that still rejects My plan.

You will know you have answered Me, because something will happen in you. As you exercise faith in Jesus, you will leave the dead idols of the old life. Your soul will be filled with hope in the expectant return of My Son. Your life will be marked by divine changes—your belief will be impacted by faith, your endurance will be inspired by hope and your reason for living will be motivated by love. When you respond to My calling, your convictions will be based on the truth of My Word.

My child, I have chosen you. I love and value you! As the focus of My love, you are called to be a free and fulfilled person. I have chosen you to be part of a faithful people. I know you by name, and I am continuing to call you deeper into Me.

I love you,
Abba

YOUR HEART

In your quiet time with God, ask Him this question: "Father, what would You like to say to me today?" Write what you believe He is saying to you. Write your name, and begin to capture whatever comes to mind, just as if God were speaking to you. For you see, He is …

Now, take a moment to write your thoughts to our Father.

Here are a few questions and suggestions to help you as you reflect upon the theme of being chosen by God:

* When you were on the playground as a child, do you recall if you were one of the first or last to be chosen for a team? How did you feel about being a part or being left out?

- When did you first hear God calling your name? Did you respond immediately or did you wait?

- How well do you hear Him calling your name today?

- As you read Ephesians chapter one, notice God's pursuit of you; how do you want to respond?

Prayer

Father, thank You for seeing me in the massive crowd of humanity. Thank You for Your unconditional love that brought Jesus here to find me. Thank You for seeing potential in me and calling my name. Thank You for the gift of faith to step out of the shadows and say, "Yes, I accept Your call ... here I am." Now, my hope is in You for the grace to live like a chosen one on The Journey. In the name of Jesus, the Chosen One, amen.

Week 7

GETTING OUT OF THE BOX

Devotional Scriptures

Isaiah 46:5–11
Hebrews 6:9–20
Matthew 19:16–30
Matthew 6:19–34
1 Corinthians 3:10–17
2 Timothy 1:1–14

The Psalmist's Pen

Psalm 45

FROM STEVE'S HEART

I really enjoy the outdoors and seem to have an appreciation for the vast array of God's creativity: mountain majesty, beach tranquility, flatland simplicity, forest celebration, or desert clarity. Although I have my preference, it's *all* pretty awesome. Perhaps the outdoors pulls on my heart because nature is such a spacious place.

It's amazing to me how God plants wild flowers where no one will see them; how waves pound the beach without fail; and how all the little sand crabs run for cover while no human eye is there to watch in amazement. From the brilliant colors of sea life to the unobservable galaxies and stars above, nature is an amazing portrait of sounds, colors, textures, and scents. God gave such thought and attention to all this and most of it will not ever be seen by man.

In light of His extravagant provision, isn't it a bit odd that we often live our lives anxious and distressed? I am beginning to realize how much we live in a box.

Do you ever try to put God in a box? One purpose of a box is to contain something. How foolish to think we could or ever would want to put God in a box! He is too infinite for the boxes of our human thinking to contain.

Once we think we've got God boxed up, we immediately put limits on our own lives. Our self-made boxes then create stress, fear, anxiety, restriction, and darkness. Of course, we are constantly tempted to put others in a box as well. Perhaps our tendency to box everyone in is the result of our being so consumed with what is here today and gone tomorrow. Or perhaps it is our constant battle with self-rule and our desire to be God.

Whatever drives this propensity to place limits on potential, God calls us to a "spacious place" (Psalm 18). Out of the box we find a life filled with possibilities and dreams that are personal and purposeful, aligned with the eternal purpose of God. I want to challenge you to step out of the box. Engage yourself in the pursuit of truth regarding what is holding you back from your full potential on The Journey.

Perhaps today you will see a snowflake falling gently to the ground or a sparrow pecking at his lunch. Maybe tomorrow you will notice that huge oak tree in its majestic splendor, or the fragrant rose in her radiant beauty. As you witness the spacious wonder of nature, remember God is also inviting you to a spacious place in His eternal purpose on The Journey.

I wonder what He wants to say to us as we contrast His care for wild flowers—temporary beauties that fade in days—with His eternal purpose for us—individuals created to live forever? Today, as you enjoy the next step in The Journey, think on God's eternal purpose for you. Believe it and rejoice!

FROM THE FATHER'S HEART

It is so easy for you to become trapped in the temporal; this is *not* the same thing as living in the moment. The Journey is to be lived in the present, for that truly is all you have. But The Journey is longer, much longer than the moment.

Human nature sees things from a short-term perspective, with a defining point to begin and end. But there is no beginning or end to Me. I *am* the Beginning and the End! Because I am God, I see things from the standpoint of eternity. My purposes will always stand. I will do what I please—what I have said I will perform, and what I have planned I will do.

For each of My children, I know the end from the beginning. And I always plan a good end for My kids. How I love to reveal My ending purposes to you!

The Journey is big-picture living that demands alignment with My purpose. People without connection to My eternal purpose make up stuff and make gods out of stuff. Stuff is temporary. The more you are tied to man-made gods, the more you will be *trapped in the temporary* instead of the eternal.

By nature, people want a god they can control—an idol that can be put in its place and is always right where they put it. They want an irresponsive being—one that won't say anything back to them, regardless of what they say to it. But hand-made, man-made gods can't *do* anything either!

I am the only one and true God. All knees will bow before Me. Everyone will say of Me, "Yes! Salvation and strength are in God!" I am the Alpha and Omega, who *was,* who *is,* and who *is to come,* the Almighty, the Eternal. I am not affected by time; I am without beginning or end.

Because you are so time-based in your worldview, you struggle to get your mind around the truth that I am not affected by time. My eternal purpose and desire is to enjoy a relationship with you today—in the *now*—and to continue our fellowship *then* when *now* is no longer. Eternity is your existence unaffected by time, without beginning or end.

My eternal agenda is for you to know My unconditional love. It grieves Me when you resist My love, and when you love yourself or other things more than Me. When you only live in the now, without a purpose for eternity, your choices become misguided and are not grounded on My eternity or My love.

When you grab hold of My eternal purpose, your life is lived intentionally with a sense of destiny, and your Journey becomes meaningful. You are released from worry because anxiety and distress are associated with a temporal life view. When you begin to see things from My perspective, your preoccupation with getting, will change to a desire to respond to My giving.

Remember, I have chosen you. Please align yourself with My eternal purpose. As you decide to live in light of eternity, your worries of tomorrow will disappear. The Journey is about living with the reality of My initiative and provision, My presence, purpose, love, and care. Quit putting Me, yourself, and others in a box. As you continue in The Journey, open your eyes to see from the viewpoint of eternity.

I love you,
Abba

YOUR HEART

In your quiet time with God, ask Him this question: "Father, what would You like to say to me today?" Write what you believe He is saying to you. Write your name, and begin to capture whatever comes to mind, just as if God were speaking to you. For you see, He is ...

Now, take a moment to write your thoughts to our Father.

Here are a few questions and suggestions to help you as you reflect upon the theme of getting out of the box:

- How have you put God in a box? What does that look like? How does that impact your relationship with Him?

- What does your box or comfort zone look like? What is holding you back from your full potential?

- How do the two concepts of temporal verses eternal impact your life? What would you ask God to do regarding your ability to live with an eternal view?

Prayer

Father, help me recognize when I begin to sacrifice the eternal on the altar of the immediate. I confess it is easy for me to get so caught up in the here *that I live like there is no* there. *Forgive me for trying to put You, myself, and others in a box. Grant me grace to embrace the spacious place you have for me. I desire and determine to schedule quiet time with you, so I may live out of the box and in the moment, keeping an eternal perspective. Capture me with Your vision. Help me make wise choices. Use me to release others to enjoy this worry-free, faith-based spacious place along The Journey. I love You. In the name of Jesus, amen.*

Week 8

FOLLOWING

Devotional Scriptures

John 1:1–51
Matthew 9:9–13
Luke 9:23–27
Matthew 10:34–42
John 10:22–30
Matthew 11:25–30
1 Corinthians 1:1–9

The Psalmist's Pen

Psalm 148

FROM STEVE'S HEART

A couple of years ago, I participated in Outward Bound Professional, a training program for executive development. Outward Bound pushes people to their limits and is designed to achieve individual transformation through challenge. This program provided a significant growth opportunity using wilderness experience with a group of strangers and minimal provisions.

We had guides for our adventure. Most of us had never really backpacked, gone rock climbing, or repelled. Success required we follow *limited* leadership. The guides were present to watch over us. Although they rarely forced our decisions, they required us to reach our destination before making camp. We enjoyed a lot of freedom while pressed to reach our goal. A life-changing experience, Outward Bound also provided me with a few lessons for my life's journey.

When I returned home, I began thinking of all the valuable insights I had learned from my wilderness experience. I then compiled a list of *Six Lessons from the Forest:*

1. The Foundation of Trust

2. The Support of Communication

3. The Power of Focus

4. The Necessity of Risk

5. The Strength of Teamwork

6. The Simplicity of Life

My experience with Outward Bound was not only an exciting adventure, but also a unique opportunity to grow in understanding of leadership. Nine strangers learned to live together, watch out for one another, and support and encourage each other. At one point, we were given a topographical map and compass, but limited knowledge regarding what was next. Ultimately, trust, communication, focus, risk, teamwork, and simplicity became very important as we learned to navigate through the wilderness to our final destination.

Through this experience, I learned that accepting unobtrusive leadership is vital to my success. Just like I had to submit to a stranger's suggestion to go east instead of west in our expedition, I also have to submit to the leadership of the Holy Spirit in my daily life. There may be times when I want to head one way, but the Lord is nudging me in another. To arrive at my final destination, I must learn to follow His leadership.

This week, I want to challenge you to evaluate what it means to follow Jesus and accept His leadership. As we accept His leadership and submit to His authority, we will reach the final destination of our Journey.

FROM THE FATHER'S HEART

Everyone is a follower of someone. Some people follow their own life script. While influenced by others, they think they can call the shots and remain firm in the seat of self-government. Control of one's life is a common illusion. Some believe a political agenda brings meaning to life. Some allow an economic interpretation to impact their decision-making. Others are guided by hatred, while others are led by their unrestrained pursuit of pleasure.

Yes, there are a lot of voices seeking your allegiance and offering to help you make sense out of life. The results vary, but without faith in My revelation, it will not work out. The question regarding life's purpose and life after life remains unanswered if you follow anyone other than Jesus.

It breaks My heart to see the pain caused by an unwillingness or failure to follow Jesus, who is the Way, the Truth, and the Life. Sent as the "Light of life," His life is your light to live by. Jesus came and lived as a man amongst men. He came as prophesied. Those who had been foretold about His coming did not take note. He came to His own people, but they did not want Him. But I have good news! *Whoever* does accept Him, *whoever* does believe He is the Son of God, *whoever* will follow Him today, will be on the path to becoming all I created them to be.

By the way, I can handle initial doubt. Remember Nathaniel's response when his brother Philip told him: "We've found the One Moses wrote of in the Law, the One the prophets spoke of for years. It's Jesus, Joseph's son, the one from Nazareth?" Nathaniel said, "Nazareth? You've got to be kidding!" It's not shocking to Me that people find it difficult to believe at first. In fact, The Journey is a progressive development of learning to believe and follow.

My Spirit reveals truth; you believe or doubt until you work it out, often the hard way. Even those committed to following Jesus have to follow. Sometimes it takes a while for you to act in agreement with what I say. Alignment of your heart with the truth comes first; then, your life is transformed by following My guidance. I want you to embrace My Word and follow My leadership in all things––forgiveness of sins, management of money, relationships, purpose, destiny, healthy lifestyle choices, and the entire experience of allowing Jesus to live through you.

Following Jesus requires you to answer the question asked of Peter: "Who do you say I am?" There are only two options—rejection (the reaction of the religious authorities), or pursuit (the response of His disciples). Who do *you* say I am? Do you comprehend the invitation to follow Me? You are prepared to follow when you say with conviction, "Jesus, I believe you are the Christ, the Messiah, and the Son of God."

It is important for you to recognize your need for Me and learn to depend on My grace. I am calling you to follow Me whether your life is easy or weary. You can try to follow religion, but it will only confuse you. You can try to control your life, but running your own show is exhausting.

I sent Jesus to make My truth clear to anyone who will listen. To those in pain and who don't have it all together, Jesus came to show restoration and recovery of life. Through Him, I am offering My peace and rest.

If you are weary, come and walk with Jesus; learn from His life and what He taught. Learn the natural rhythm of living in My grace—it's My gift. Learn to know Me, and you'll discover I will not place anything too heavy on you without also providing the ability to respond. Jesus will teach you how to live life careless in My care.

You are outward bound—I will never give up on you on this spiritual adventure. Will you trust Me? Will you focus on our relationship? Will you risk loving me? Will you accept My encouragement through others? Will you let me teach you about the simplicity of life?

The Journey is quite an adventure, but I am here with unobtrusive leadership to keep you on track. My goal is to help you reach your destination; we will be face-to-face. There is no end to the work I have begun in you as a follower. Christ is in you, the Hope of My glory.

I love you,
Abba

YOUR HEART

In your quiet time with God, ask Him this question: "Father, what would You like to say to me today?" Write what you believe He is saying to you. Write your name, and begin to capture whatever comes to mind, just as if God were speaking to you. For you see, He is …

Now, take a moment to write your thoughts to our Father.

Here are a few questions and suggestions to help you as you reflect upon this idea of Following:

- Throughout Scripture people were confronted with the decision to follow Jesus. What have you sacrificed to follow Him?

- Why do you think some people choose to follow Jesus while others do not?

- How might God use your life to help others see the benefit of following Jesus?

Prayer

Our Father, thank You for calling us to follow Jesus. Thank You for sending Him to reveal Your character, Your heart, and Your ways. Forgive me for the times I have tried to follow from a distance. Thank You for the peace, grace, and rest that are mine when I choose to follow Jesus. Help me to want to follow closely. Give me grace to cooperate. Lead the way. In the name of Jesus, amen.

Week 9

GOD'S CALL

Devotional Scriptures

Luke 5:1–11
John 21
Jeremiah 1:1–19
Romans 1:1–7
1 Peter 1:1–25; 3:8–12
John 21:12–23
Mark 1:14–20

The Psalmist's Pen

Psalm 131

FROM STEVE'S HEART

Have you ever noticed the anticipation and excitement of expectant parents? For nine months, they are planning every little detail of the baby's arrival. Their whole world revolves around the new little family member to come. Tiny clothes, bottles, packages of diapers, baby furniture, soft blankets, and fuzzy teddy bears begin to fill up the house. Regular doctor visits are scheduled. Conversations are filled with the wonder of newborns. Months tick by … then weeks … then days … until finally, the moment a new little baby enters the world has come. Within minutes, the parents name the infant, giving this precious little soul a way to be recognized and called in the world.

Since the day you were born, others have called you by your name. Family, friends, teachers, neighbors—all use your name while talking to you, disciplining you, teaching you, or learning from you. As you get older, you begin to recognize other voices calling your name—work, duty, family, entertainment, the world. Some of these voices are noble, encouraging you to explore, rest, share, learn, and grow. Other voices detract you from your course, offering seasonable pleasure and worldly contentment.

With all the voices in the world pulling for our presence and attention, we wonder which ones we should heed and which ones we should ignore. The awakening continues with challenging questions: *Will I learn to listen and develop a finely attuned ear in the midst of all the voices? Will I discern which voice to listen to? When the time comes and God's call quietly enters my space, how will I respond?*

Responses vary, but they are not optional—either we seek to quiet ourselves in order to hear His voice better, or we turn up the noise of living in an effort to silence His loving call for allegiance. Realistically, I suppose most of us respond in both ways along The Journey.

Our experience on The Journey is impacted by how we respond to God's call on our lives. His call to you began when He created you in the secret place of your mother's womb. He knew you and loved you from the moment you were conceived. He quietly calls your name in the midst of so much noise and so many voices. Among all the other calls in life, His calling is centered in His love.

FROM THE FATHER'S HEART

Let Me be your peace on The Journey. Live in dependence upon Me, and I will help you live well. The relationship I offer—when pursued seriously—results in your transformation into the likeness of Jesus. The expression of Christ's likeness is not limited to a particular role, profession, or assignment. Letting the life of Jesus be manifest in your mortal body is the call for all My children.

Don't expect Me to force you or plead with you. When I call, it is without irresistible pressure. My call comes to the receptive. The passionate call of Jesus to follow Him is gently spoken. Whether you hear or not depends on the condition of your head. Your heart, more than your mind, is what allows you to listen. A right heart will recognize I have chosen you for an intimate relationship through Jesus Christ.

Yes, the initial call is to repent of your sins and follow Jesus, but there is so much more. My intent is that you reflect the life of Jesus in your everyday experience. The Journey is about growing up, following, and reflecting Jesus regardless of your role or lot in life. A heart after Me is My grace gift to you. This attitude of heart combined with your availability to listen allows you to hear My call.

The original disciples were fishermen by trade. Every time they listened to Jesus' advice, they caught fish. But He called them to something higher—He called them to be fishers of men. To follow Jesus is not about your profession or your place in life. Whether you refuse or fail to follow, the call to follow Me is always present everyday with every decision.

All around voices are calling you, summoning you to join a group, a cause, a destiny, or an identity. But I, God Almighty, am calling you to align yourself to My purposes. Your response to My call determines the quality, purpose, and impact of your life. Because My call is vital to your destiny, it grieves Me when you put My call on hold.

When you call out for help, I am here to give you assistance. Too often you call out for help knowing you will slide back into old self-destructive patterns of thought and behavior. I want you to keep pursuing My call on a daily basis. My call keeps you focused all through life on the big picture. My call to live as a follower of Jesus does not allow you to do whatever you feel like doing all the time. You must remain disciplined and determined to daily answer My call. Set your hope on what you know and believe while anticipating Jesus' return.

Your life is a journey—live it with an attentiveness and consciousness of Me. It cost the precious blood of Jesus to rescue you from the dead-end, empty-headed life you grew up in before your awakening. My heart is calling for your total commitment as well. I love you endlessly and desire what is best for you. In love and commitment, answer My call with all your heart.

I love you,
Abba

YOUR HEART

In your quiet time with God, ask Him this question: "Father, what would You like to say to me today?" Write what you believe He is saying to you. Write your name, and begin to capture whatever comes to mind, just as if God were speaking to you. For you see, He is…

Now, take a moment to write your thoughts to our Father.

Here are a few questions to aid you in following God's call amidst all the other voices in the world:

- Who are some of the loudest voices in your world? What are they calling for, wanting from you? How are you responding to them?

- Which voices could lead you away from God's path for your life? What steps are you taking to minimize their influence?

- When do you take time to listen for the voice of God? Are you satisfied with that effort? What would need to change for that time alone to improve? Why would that be a good thing?

Prayer

Our Father, thank You for loving me so much that You have called me to You. Grant me a desire to be still and grace to listen for Your voice in the midst of all the noise and voices around me. Give me a heart after You. Here I am, help me commit my life to You and Your call on my life. Lead the way. In the name of Jesus, amen.

Week 10

GOD'S POWERFUL WORD

Devotional Scriptures

John 1:1–13
Genesis 1:1–31
Matthew 9:1–8
Luke 1:26–38
Philippians 1:6–7
2 Timothy 3:16–17

The Psalmist's Pen

Psalm 29

FROM STEVE'S HEART

A few years ago, I attended a luncheon where Tim Russert, the moderator and managing editor of *Meet the Press,* spoke. You may recall Russert's use of the white dry eraser board on election night 2000 as he tried to explain what was going on in Florida—it made *TV Guide's 100 Most Memorable TV Moments.* The Washington Post credits him with coining the phrase "Red State" and "Blue State" to explain the nation's political divide. He was an anchor on MSNBC and CNBC, as well as senior vice president and Washington bureau chief for NBC news. His career highlights as a journalist are impressive. Prior to the luncheon, he spoke to some 1,700 people on world events, national matters, and political topics.

But it was his comments at the luncheon that most impressed me, for there his words became powerful. The motivation behind his books *Big Russ and Me* and *Wisdom of Our Fathers: Lessons and Letters from Daughters and Sons* emerged. His first book had an amazing affect on relationships in America, while his second book is evidence of the impact. As he took questions, he shared stories about his mother and father, his education in a Catholic school, and his family. It was at that point that I began to understand why he was named the 1995 Father of the Year by the National Father's Day Committee and why *Parents* magazine honored him as Dream Dad in 1998.

Although I don't know him up close and personal, I caught a glimpse of his heart that day as his stories revealed his respect for his parents, the context of his early education, and his commitment as a dad. I left the luncheon with his words resonating in my mind. The words he had spoken were not only insightful and encouraging, but they also became powerful in my life.

One of Russert's stories especially stuck with me. One day his wife, Maureen, informed him that their son Luke had a tattoo. Immediately, he called Luke in and began to question him. His initial reaction was to ask "What were you thinking?" He reminded Luke of how they had discussed the health risks and that this behavior was unacceptable. He finally demanded to see the tattoo.

After considerable resistance, Luke raised his shirt to reveal three small letters "TJR" tattooed on his side. Hear Luke's explanation: "Dad I always wanted you and Grandpa on my side." The three letters were indeed the initials of Timothy John Russert, Sr. and Timothy John Russert, Jr. Stunned, Tim Russert pulled himself together only to say, "That's a great looking tattoo, son!"

In a grace-filled moment, Russert's story became God's word to me—the words took on power as the Holy Spirit breathed life into them. One of my commitments and goals is to be a spiritual leader for my family, and part of my journey is learning to effectively perform that calling. The moment I heard this renowned journalist's story, I was immediately inspired in my role to be like Jesus in my home. My desire and commitment to "be present" and more fully connected with our daughters and their husbands and our grandchildren was enlarged that afternoon.

The Journey requires us to listen to God—whether His written Word or words inspired by the Holy Spirit—in order to be transformed. This week, I challenge you to listen closely as the Holy Spirit speaks to you. May you be changed by God's powerful Word.

FROM THE FATHER'S HEART

My Word was spoken into the darkness, the nothingness, and emptiness of earth. I spoke and brought forth beauty and wonder. I created everything you can see—from the fathomless oceans, majestic mountains, and dense forests to millions of animals and the starry night sky. I even created things that you can't see like the wind and the atomic world. It was My power, My spoken word that brought everything into existence.

My Word was spoken to the heart of a young woman named Mary. As she believed, I brought forth My Son, Jesus. His birth was the result of My power and not human conception.

Some thirty-three years after He was born, Jesus was crucified, died, and was buried. Three days later, He was raised from the dead. It was My power that resurrected Him.

My Word has power to create and transform. I convert chaos into order and beauty, darkness into light and life, despair into hope and confidence. With My power, failure is changed to growth and maturity, and fear to peace and rest. My Word turns brokenness into compassion and commitment. All that I speak is good. Everything I say comes from a heart of love that is not self-motivated, but has only your best in mind.

The battle for your ears is as great as the battle for your heart. Are you willing to listen—still and attentive—to Me? Will you rest and know that I am God?

My Word has the ability to make things happen. In creation I said, "Let there be light!" and light appeared. I called forth the night and day, and they came to be. Over and over I spoke and My word performed—Sky! Land! Sea Life! Birds! Animals! The crowning moment came when I said, "Let's make human beings in Our image," and then My very own special creation, man, came into existence.

Notice the difference between man's abusive authority and My love-guided authority. In Matthew 9:1–8, Jesus forgave the sins of the young paraplegic boy. Accusing Him of blasphemy, the religious scholars rejected Him as the Son of God. But Jesus only spoke and confirmed His authority as He demonstrated His identity by healing the boy's broken body. Some of those who witnessed this miracle believed, while others became more rigid in their rejection of My love-motivated authority.

I want you to understand that power is the ability and capacity to get something done. At Creation, the earth's nothingness provided Me plenty of room to speak My Word and call creation into being. Mary's total trust and complete submission allowed Me to move in her life and bring My Son into history. The complete obedience of Jesus—to the point of death on a cross—allowed Me to raise Him from the grave and complete My plan for your salvation.

When you allow Me to move, My power comes in and enlarges your capacity to be who I created you to be. The power of My Word is released so you can live well, whole, and healthy, free and joyous. When you become available to Me and obey My Word, My power will complete the work I began in you. Through My Word, you are put together and shaped for your tasks. Every part of My Word is useful—it shows you truth, exposes rebellion, and corrects mistakes. As My word trains you to live My way, it empowers you to reach your journey's destination.

I love you,
Abba

YOUR HEART

In your quiet time with God, ask Him this question: "Father, what would You like to say to me today?" Write what you believe He is saying to you. Write your name, and begin to capture whatever comes to mind, just as if God were speaking to you. For you see, He is ...

Now, take a moment to write your thoughts to our Father.

Here are a few questions and suggestions to help you as you reflect upon the theme of God's powerful Word:

- Write down the word heart. What words do you see within the word?

- Okay, if you don't like word puzzles there are two words: "ear" and "hear." Now, what connection do you make between ears, hear, and heart as it concerns your relationship with God? With His Word?

- How strong is your desire for God's Word? What would you like it to be? What can you do to get there?

Prayer

Father, with faith in Your Son, Jesus, I embrace the authority of Scripture in my life. I need the power of Your Word in my life so I may glorify You. My ambition is to live my life pleasing to You. Grant me grace to desire and listen to Your Word. Help me to develop my capacity to be like Jesus by the power of Your Word until the day of His appearing. In Jesus' name, amen.

Week 11

THE ADVENTURE

Devotional Scriptures

Luke 14:1–14
Luke 14:25–34
Luke 9:57–62
Philippians 2:1–11
John 6:60–71
Acts 4:32–37
Romans 15:1–13

The Psalmist's Pen

Psalm 32

FROM STEVE'S HEART

Have you ever watched *Mission Impossible* or another international espionage movie? These Hollywood blockbusters are full of intrigue, adventure, and suspense. Within two hours of film, the hero is chased by speeding cars, shot at by dangerous men in black, escapes nuclear explosions, nearly drowns in a shark tank, and survives a helicopter crash in some Middle Eastern country—all during his effort to complete a top-secret mission. It's not until the end of the 120-minute cinematic production of drama and special effects that you can calmly sit in your chair, relieved that the hero successfully finished his mission and still had all limbs intact.

Most of us have, at some time or another, dreamed of a life of adventure—a chance to fight through enemy lines for a sacred mission. We would summon all our courage, bravado, and honor to face the darkness bravely and achieve victory. Our heroics would not only serve our country, but also save the entire world from certain destruction!

Now close your eyes for a moment, and imagine yourself in one of these movies. Imagine the call comes to your high-tech global cell phone (cue *Mission Impossible* music). On the other line is a muffled voice telling you of a great mission that has been assigned to you. Your ability to accomplish this mission will impact the course of history. To insure the successful outcome of your assignment, you need qualified individuals who will risk all and align themselves with you.

Since time is of the essence, you immediately begin the task of recruiting your team. You find your first potential undercover agent and begin pitching him the assignment. He is all in—until he learns that he'll be sleeping in the back of a sheep truck in Yemen instead of a five-star hotel in Paris. So you continue your search. You find another candidate, but to your chagrin, he can't accompany you either.

"I have a family funeral to attend," this one replies. "Get back to me in a few days."

You meet a third possibility, but he too has other commitments. "I'm ready to join you on your mission," he says, "but I've got several appointments already scheduled in my planner."

Dismayed, you cry, "There's no time to put this off! We have to complete the mission now!"

From this scenario, you can imagine both the desire and intensity to find people who would join you on your very important mission. This quest for followers is a picture of Jesus' own search for disciples. He is looking for others to join Him on the kingdom's assignment. He is scouring the earth for hearts that would forsake all and follow Him. Too many have other priorities and excuses, but He is searching for individuals who will put Him first and say, "Regardless of the cost, I will go!"

The Journey is not about what you do with Jesus' teachings and resurrection only, but what you do with His mission as well. His mission demands allegiance and total commitment. As you progress in The Journey, you are called to the life-long pursuit of an ever-deepening relationship with Jesus.

As you read the Scripture this week, consider the request Jesus asks of you to be His disciple. Are you willing to lay aside your time, ideas, and earthly priorities to follow Him? In addition to seeking to know Him, will you also seek to live the life He requires?

FROM THE FATHER'S HEART

As you continue in your Journey, I want you to know that I am always committed to you. I will counsel and coach you, watch carefully over you, and lead you along the right path. Although I am always here for you, you have to decide if and how you will respond to Me. The more accessible you are to Me, the more effective your Journey will be. It is My desire that you live in My unfailing love and place your trust in Me.

I have so many wonderful things planned for you, but as you are beginning to realize, this life is not your own. I am calling you to a higher level in Me, and this requires true discipleship. If you want to truly follow Me, become My disciple. To determine where you are on the road of discipleship, ask yourself these three questions.

First, who is the master of your life? This reveals your source of truth and authority, for no person can have two masters. Are you ready and willing to accept My Word? Do you believe Jesus is who He said He is? Do you believe He was born of a virgin, died for your sins, and rose from the dead? Do you long for His return? Are you embracing His authority in your life today?

Secondly, are you totally available? This addresses the call to duty. Are you functioning as a disciple in your choices and life roles? Or are your words failing to be supported by actions? The mission is demanding and the battle fierce. The enemy puts up a good fight, and the distractions are relentless. A disciple believes what the Master teaches and is called upon to spread the Good News like a farmer scattering his seed. Your life is to be fruitful. As you avail yourself to Me, others will see the Master in you and learn of the Truth.

Thirdly, will you let go of everything in order to follow? Total abandonment is required. You must be willing to take what is dearest to you—plans, people, or possessions—and give it all to Me.

In becoming a disciple, pattern yourself after the Master. In every way, He is your example—even in discipleship. Jesus had equal status with Me, but He put aside His self-interest, letting go of the advantages His position provided to Him. He set aside the privileges of deity and took on the very nature and the role of a servant. It was a humbling experience, yet He fully obeyed. Instead of focusing on His personal comfort or agenda, He focused on redemption, paying the ultimate price of death.

Any true disciple of Jesus follows His example. So pick up your cross and follow Him. Let go of everything, be totally available, and trust Me to do what is best with your life offering.

There have always been various responses to this call. Discipleship *is* costly, but the reward and impact far exceeds the sacrifice. To live a selfless, love-inspired, and purpose driven life is My gift to all who follow. To share the message with others is the privilege of all disciples and the adventure.

I love you,
Abba

YOUR HEART

In your quiet time with God, ask Him this question: "Father, what would You like to say to me today?" Write what you believe He is saying to you. Write your name, and begin to capture whatever comes to mind, just as if God were speaking to you. For you see, He is…

Now, take a moment to write your thoughts to our Father.

Here are a few questions and suggestions to help you as you reflect upon the theme of The Adventure:

- What image comes to mind when you think of following Jesus? What does that say to you?

- How adventurous are you? How might your relationship with God be impacted if you thought of the Christian Life as an adventure? Do you?

- What do you think would need to happen for you to be a fully engaged, passionate follower of Jesus?

- What would it cost you? How prepared are you to lay it all on the line for Jesus?

Prayer

Father, I renew my commitment to Jesus as Master. Here am I; use my life to advance Your kingdom and glorify Your Name. I place my trust in You as I let go of everything to pick up my cross and follow Jesus. As I go into my every day, ordinary life I pledge my personal allegiance to You. My ambition is to be pleasing to You and to help others come to know You. In Jesus' name, amen.

Week 12
CHOOSING LIFE

Devotional Scriptures

Matthew 7:1–14
Ephesians 4:1–8
Philippians 3:8–21
Luke 12:22–34
1 Thessalonians 4:1–18
1 Corinthians 15:1–58

The Psalmist's Pen

Psalm 51

FROM STEVE'S HEART

Recently, I attended the Oral Roberts University luncheon at the Ignite Leadership Conference Luncheon where John Maxwell was guest speaker. As a highly recognized motivational speaker, Maxwell is known for his insight into business leadership, teamwork, and influence. During this particular luncheon, he spoke on four things that lead to "REAL" success. The points were discussed in the acronym REAL:

Relationships—getting along with and adding value to others

Equipping—building a team

Attitude—changing your thinking

Leadership—ability to exert influence

While enlightening us on the route to real success, Maxwell recounted a story about an elder in a small remote village. Someone had asked the elder if any great men were born in that village. The elder had replied, "No, just babies." Maxwell pointed out that leadership is not based on birth, but on desire. He stated, "The moment you are born, you begin to make choices, and those choices make you. If you want to be a great leader, you have to make the choice to become one."*

Everyone has the power of choice regardless of gender, age, or status. In fact, God gave mankind the freedom of choice when He created Adam. Life is a pattern of choices, and your everyday choices determine who you are and who you become. Your reach of influence—and hence your leadership ability—is determined by the choices you make today.

We are faced with choices every step of the Journey. Our lives move with every decision; we either choose life or death, blessing or curse. Our choices impact the life or death of a dream, a relationship, a family, a business, our purpose in life, and our eternal destiny. Starting today, let's make the decision to aggressively choose life!

FROM THE FATHER'S HEART

At the dawn of creation, I gave mankind the freedom of choice. You can choose right or wrong, darkness or light, life or death. Your choices can maximize or minimize your potential, enhance or hinder your opportunities, or move you toward or away from Me. I do not force man to do anything—I gave him the power to choose for himself.

The first choice I place before you is to believe that Jesus died for your sins. I have revealed Him to the world as My Son. He lived a pure life, was crucified, and buried, but rose again. This is eternity in reality, but you have the choice to believe it. Your response to this truth impacts the rest of your existence! This is where you begin to choose life, for all other life choices flow out of this foundational reality.

Once you choose Jesus as the Way to life, you enter into relationship with Me. The Good News shows you how to move from spiritual death to life in Christ. Regardless of the trends and teachings of man, Jesus is the only option. Here is your choice: what will you do with Jesus? To choose life is to believe the resurrection of Jesus. If you don't believe this, there is no basis for any hope of eternal life, just different interpretations regarding your experience of life on earth.

So what do you believe? Who is Jesus Christ? Did He really die and come back to life? Once you settle this question and choose to believe, you lay the foundation for your spiritual existence. If there is no resurrection, then it is foolish to place your faith in Christ for the forgiveness of sins. Without the resurrection, Christianity is just a religion void of divine power.

Life is more than your physical and mental experience—it is a spiritual principle. Life is existence transcending death. To choose life, you must choose to believe in Jesus—His life, death, and resurrection.

When I created the first man, Adam, I gave him the choice of obedience. Through his wrongful choice, he brought death to the human race. Through My Son Jesus, I gave humanity a second chance—and another opportunity to choose life. Those who choose to believe Him become spiritually alive. Your natural life does not get you into My kingdom; the nature of your earthly flesh is death. Life comes from Christ. Once you choose life in Christ, your Journey begins. The choices you make from this moment on can bring you into alignment with My purpose and carry you into abundant life.

At every turn, you are faced with a host of alternatives. Every day you make hundreds of choices, all impacting your existence. In the simplest sense, life is narrowly defined as the interval between birth and death. This shortsighted perspective impacts your choices.

If you consider only the present, your choices will become self-centered, creating a journey that is less than intended.

Please open up to Me regarding everything in your life. I want to help you live a focused life and make better choices. Yes, there are many paths to choose from, some of which are not pleasing to Me. But as you embrace Jesus and My plan for your existence, you will move toward your greatest fulfillment and success.

My child, how I love you! I desire to be fully engaged in your everyday ordinary life. I anticipate the day your earthly body will be transformed into a glorious body, and we stand face-to-face. Let this hope be real as you embrace My Son Jesus Christ.

So what do you want? Your choices define your place in human history. Your willingness to choose Me impacts both your earthly and eternal life. Keep focused on the goal to achieve your full potential and become everything you were created to be. Pursue a life of wonder, faith, love, steadiness, and courtesy. Run hard and fast in the faith. Embrace My salvation and choose life.

I love you,
Abba

YOUR HEART

In your quiet time with God, ask Him this question: "Father, what would You like to say to me today?" Write what you believe He is saying to you. Write your name, and begin to capture whatever comes to mind, just as if God were speaking to you. For you see, He is ...

Now, take a moment to write your thoughts to our Father.

Here are a few questions and suggestions to help you as you reflect upon the theme of choosing life:

- As you examine your recent choices, how have your decisions been made? What were they based on?

- What choices are you making today to support your relationship with God and your spiritual development?

- What choices are you making today that may be the biggest threat to your relationship with God? With others? For your health? Your future? What needs to change?

Prayer

Father, I admit my choices fall short of the love-based response I want to give You. Forgive me. Help me live in alignment with Your calling, the hope of eternal life, and the wisdom of Your Word so I make better choices. Grant me grace to live aware of choices that impact my life, my witness, and the lives of those around me. In Jesus' name, amen.

*Reference John Maxwell- Talent is Never Enough

Week 13

GOD'S ABUNDANT MERCY

Devotional Scriptures

> 1 Peter 1:3; 2:1–10
> Jeremiah 3:1–14
> Lamentation 5
> Luke 1:46–56
> Isaiah 63–66
> James 2:1–13
> Luke 6:27–36
> Proverbs 28:13

The Psalmist's Pen

> Psalm 116

FROM STEVE'S HEART

We were living in the Panhandle of Oklahoma; it was a hot summer's night. As a young couple we sat on the front step of a small cement slab covered with well-worn brown outdoor carpet. You could call it the "front porch" if you use your imagination and didn't want the comfort of a chair.

The small white frame house was isolated from other residents. On the south was the local lumberyard, First Baptist Church was just across the alley to the west, the Nazarene church was next door on the east, and the telephone mechanical house and Pizza Hut were across the street to the south.

The small front porch was attached to the parsonage; the parsonage was located next door to the church where I was pastor in Beaver, Oklahoma. This small town was the county seat and located in the panhandle. Most of the locals seemed to embrace the well-worn descriptor, "No Man's Land."

We arrived as a young couple as the *next* new parsonage family August 2, 1982. Our third daughter was born October 10, as an Okie (her sisters were born in Independence, Kansas and Baton Rouge, Louisiana). We were a picture perfect young family: three little girls, a beautiful wife, and handsome husband.

Although I had served as an associate pastor, this was my first senior pastor assignment. The previous two years I had returned to college with my family to finish my bachelor's degree. Now I was eager, excited, and committed to my call, the work, and to growing my first church—located in "No Man's Land."

On this particular summer night, our three little girls were in bed as we found ourselves sitting on the "front porch" in "No Man's Land." The moment, unannounced had arrived for one of those life-changing chats, along the journey.

Do you get the picture? Mother of three under the age of four, wife to an over-committed pastor-husband determined to change the world by changing the mindset of a small church in a small town in "No Man's Land."

Although my motives were pure, and my commitment genuine I was about to learn an important lesson. Rita, as a young wife and mother had been separated from family support for five years; finances were minimal, and the neighborhood and schedule did not provide weekly tea parties.

It was a hot summer night when we sat down on the front step for a conversation. Without warning the conversation became real. The exact words don't matter. The message blew me away: Rita told me how she felt, how she thought she could just walk away from it all—including *me*.

At that time of my life, I believed I was the best husband and dad on the planet, doing the work of God—who wouldn't want me on their team? So this moment of unguarded, desperate, enlightening communication knocked me off my horse. And yes, Rita had my full attention … and rightfully so.

That moment was a mercy of God moment. By His grace and with the guidance of my helpmate I began making some changes. *Wakeup calls are evidence of God's mercy.*

You have to know that my goal was not to under support my wife and mother of our three children. My intent was not to drag her away from her family and fail to provide the emotional support she needed living in a parsonage in "No Man's Land." But it became apparent that my actions betrayed my heart and intent; I needed mercy.

It would not be the last wake up call, but by God's mercy and grace, we are each other's best friend. By the mercy of God we have celebrated thirty-three years on The Journey, and we don't have enough time together.

Life requires God's mercy as we take The Journey following Jesus. Life relationships require us to offer mercy as followers of Jesus. How thankful I am for God's mercy!

THE FATHER'S HEART

Who desires mercy? Who needs it? Who stands before a judge and pleads for mercy? The person who has gone against what is acceptable by law or authority, been found guilty, and left with no recourse but to plead for compassion, kindness, leniency … mercy.

Mercy is available when you are in distress and need forgiveness, when guilty. Mercy is My kind and compassionate treatment; My gracious favor extended to you when you really have no right to claim for such favorable treatment.

When will you recognize the abundance of My mercy? When

you are willing to acknowledge the depth of your need. Then you might cry out for mercy and only those who cry out find it.

It was a difficult time for all of us, as I endured the spiritual adultery of My people and the necessity of bringing judgment upon them. The desperate condition of My people was brought on by their rejection of Me and My plan that was designed for their good. Yet, they worshipped what was not divine, not worthy of their love and devotion.

Death is separation from Me, for I am Life. Spiritual death comes to all who resist My love and rebel against My redemptive plan. I want you to understand your desperate need for mercy. Justice is satisfied only when by My mercy you are made right with Me through Jesus Christ. Your wholehearted love is My desire—a living sacrifice.

Yes, it is a journey, but I want you to hunger and thirst for righteousness, for life over death. Every choice moves you closer to life or death. Decisions, choices that appeal to your flesh, move you towards death, while decisions, choices that are truth-based, love-motivated, and obedient to My Word and alignment with Jesus, move you towards life. Mercy meets you on the road to death and allows you to receive life.

See My mercy extended to you through Jesus crucified on the cross. See it. Look at the cross. See Him. Do you understand your need for kind and compassionate treatment? Do you comprehend My plan to forgive your sins and give you life? Do you trust Me to love you as the giver of mercy?

Frankly, the lip service so often offered up offends Me. I'm God, the one true God of all Creation; it is My breath that is in you. Halfhearted responses sicken Me as they destroy and rob you of your vitality, hope, passion, and love for Me. It is your well being that I have in mind.

Please recognize My offer of mercy, seek My face, and I will come to revive and refresh, to restore your experience of being. I will lift you up. Receive My compassion and forgiveness … My love poured out to all who fear Me, from one generation to another.

Notice and rehearse the things I have done; things demonstrating My mercy in history.

Do you re-call when I showed you mercy? Do you understand that mercy is My love and goodness in action even while you were guilty, miserable, and misguided? I offer mercy to alleviate your distress and show you my heart in your time of need. Yes, if you are rebellious and shut Me out, I will still reach out. Mercy is about bringing you relief. I love being merciful!

Now, as it relates to your relationships with other people, follow My lead. I am kind to the ungrateful and wicked. Mercy is about living generously, not with a get-even attitude. You'll never regret living your life and treating others the way I handle you—generous and gracious even when under serving. I am merciful; follow My lead.

What's the point of jumping on the failure of others? What gain is in criticizing? Do you want that? How does it help to condemn someone who is already down; would you like such hardness? Be kind and merciful, easy on others, and your life will be a lot easier, too.

Sure, relationships can be challenging; that's why I teach and empower you to love your enemies. This brings the best out of you instead of reactions that take you down a level. Someone is giving you a hard time? Bring them to Me in prayer; let's work on this together...starting with you. Mercy allows you to live freely, relate to others generously, and handle them as you would like to be handled.

So, how do you receive mercy?

Acknowledge, confess, and renounce your sins.

This is how you correct the *consequences of your life:* confess to Me where you are, admit your need, own your stuff; turn away from the old ways and cry out for forgiveness...for My help. What happens? My love, dressed as mercy, comes running to where you are, and I minister to your need until you find relief.

It is My heart's desire to alleviate your distress and offer com-

passion along The Journey. So few cry out for My mercy. Do you know why? They refuse to acknowledge their need.

How may I help you today?

I love you,
Abba

YOUR HEART

In your quiet time with God, ask Him this question: "Father, what would You like to say to me today?" Write what you believe He is saying to you. Write your name, and begin to capture whatever comes to mind, just as if God were speaking to you. For you see, He is …

Now, take a moment to write your thoughts to our Father.

Here are a few questions to help you as you reflect upon God's Mercy:

- When were you deeply aware of God's mercy?

- What would you like to say to God about His mercy?

- Where in your life do you need to cry out for God's mercy today?

- How well does the concept of mercy show up in your life and relationships? Who would benefit from you extending them mercy today?

Prayer

Merciful Father, if it were not for Your mercy I would be lost in sin and destined for a life of confusion and aimless wandering. Thank You for Your abundant grace and mercy; I cannot imagine life where there is no mercy, especially Your mercy. As I go from this place may I not only continue to recognize my need for mercy, confessing and renouncing my sins, but demonstrate mercy to those individuals needing mercy today. Amen.

Week 14

YOUR LIFE AS A SEED

Devotional Scriptures

Luke 16:1–13
Matthew 20:20–28, 29–34
Philippians 2:1–11
Hebrews 12:12–17
1 Peter 4:1–11
John 12:20–36

The Psalmist's Pen

Psalm 19 and 91

FROM STEVE'S HEART

Spring is my favorite time of year. The sun comes out from hiding, the weather is pleasant, and life is bursting forth everywhere. Trees replace their winter brown with vibrant green, birds sing their various melodies, and splashes of color return with the first yellow daffodils. The entire world is resplendent in the fragrant beauty of new life.

As spring draws nearer, the earth and its inhabitants prepare for the new season. Eggs are kept warm until hatching, cocoons are reaching their maximum incubation, flowerbeds are weeded and tilled, and the garden plot is prepped for planting. Everyone and everything is busy getting ready for birth and growth.

Prior to spring's full bloom, Rita and I enjoy working in our yard. It's fascinating watching life manifest from seed and soil. Both of us take pride in the sense of accomplishment we feel after planting seeds, caring for the young plants, or mowing the lawn.

One of life's simple delights is watching the landscape mature over the weeks. Plants grow from little six-pack starters dotting the bed to a carpet of fragrance and beauty. Dormant perennials come to life with tips of green pushing through last year's glory. The cucumber, squash, and okra seed that was once buried in the dark soil breaks through with tiny shoots peeking over mounds of dirt.

These little seeds take quite a journey from the seed packet to the burial plot in the garden and then to the dinner table. Unless these seeds are sown into the ground and allowed to take root and grow, they will never become the ripe vegetable the packet label describes. If I left all the seed packets in my garage and never planted them, these seeds would never reach their potential. Until I'm ready to let go of those seeds, there is no transformation, no delicious fruit, and no abundant life.

The Journey is much like these little packets of seeds. The seeds represent our lives, while the picture on the packet—which shows us who and what we are to become—is Jesus. For us to grow, mature, and reach our full potential in Christ, we must first release control and bury ourselves in Christ. When we die to self, die to self-preservation, we are then raised to new life, and transformed into His likeness.

During your Journey this week, I encourage you to see yourself as a seed of Christ, sown into His soil and nurtured under His care. As you surrender all to the Lord, you will begin transforming into His likeness!

FROM THE FATHER'S HEART

Today, I want you to understand the connection between rest and the place where you dwell. You can either reside in the world, facing life with your strength and ability, or you can dwell in My presence, living in the realm of My grace. I offer you the choice to come away from the world and reside under the shadow of My wing. As your shelter, I offer you protection, comfort, and peace. Will you accept My invitation to dwell in Me?

You will find rest when you dwell in the reality of My presence. If you stay connected to Me, you will find relief and freedom from the stress of everyday life. Worries will disappear, and anxiety will disintegrate once you realize I am here to care for you. When you are dwelling with Me in that secret place, your heart will sing, "The Lord is my refuge, my fortress, my God, in whom I lean on and rely upon, in whom I trust" (Psalm 91:1–2).

As you walk this Journey, learn to follow the example of Jesus. He is the picture of what you are to become. If you truly want to grow into your full potential, surrender every corner of your heart to My Lordship. Remember that a seed by itself simply remains a single seed with potential. But when a single seed is buried in the ground, life sprouts and reproduces itself many, many times over.

If you hold onto selfishness, self-promotion, and self-preservation, your life will remain a single seed and ultimately self-destruct. When you bury your life in Jesus, in total abandonment you will find the life you were truly meant to live.

Laying down your will ultimately results in salvation. Jesus' life is a perfect picture of surrender and new life. Instead of forsaking the cross and pursuing His own plan, He surrendered His will to Mine and laid down His life for humanity. Stripping Himself of all the glories of heaven, He became a servant and paid the penalty for eternity. The sacrifice of His life not only resulted in His divine resurrection, but also in the salvation of mankind. As you live in total abandonment to Me, your service will result in more than your own salvation—it will also impact others for eternity.

As you sow your life as a seed unto Me, you will steadily grow and mature into the fullness of Christ's life. Your thoughts will begin to resemble My thoughts, your actions will start to look like My actions, and your words will begin to sound like My Words. Of course, reaching your full potential in Christ is a process. Like the tiny shoots of green that peek through the earth during spring, the fruit of your new life will blossom blade by blade, and leaf by leaf. Be patient during the growing seasons and allow My Spirit to work in you. Guard your heart from parasites that will try to demolish your growth. Nurture your spirit with My Word and soak in the sunshine of My presence.

Continue along The Journey with Me, and be conscientious of the seed that is your life. Sow unto Me, and I will bring a harvest in you!

I love you,
Abba

YOUR HEART

In your quiet time with God, ask Him this question: "Father, what would You like to say to me today?" Write what you believe He is saying to you. Write your name, and begin to capture whatever comes to mind, just as if God were speaking to you. For you see, He is …

Now, take a moment to write your thoughts to our Father.

Here are a couple of questions to help you reflect on Your Life as a Seed:

- What is most encouraging to you from reading this week's thoughts?

- What if for fun you plant a seed? What do you notice?

- How could you sow into the lives of others? What can you do just for today?

Prayer

Faithful Father, open my eyes to see how I can sow My life unto You. As Jesus laid down His life to give live, so I give My life to You. Here I am a single seed. I release my life to You. As a follower of Jesus, I desire to serve You. I know that by losing my life to You, I will find it. Help me to be sensitive to Your leading to serve others with pure motives today. In Jesus' name, amen.

Week 15

THE PROMISES OF GOD

Devotional Scriptures

1 Kings 8:22–30
Nehemiah 9:6–25
Romans 4:16–25
James 1:1–15
2 Corinthians 1:12–22
2 Peter 3:5–13
Philippians 3:12–4:1

The Psalmist's Pen

Psalm 119:33–48

FROM STEVE'S HEART

Have you ever heard someone say, "I promise" only to be unable to fulfill the desired outcome? The problem was not that the outcome was inappropriate; the person just could not deliver. The situation was out of the person's control.

A promise requires more than saying words someone wants or even needs to hear. A promise demands an ability to get it done.

In December 2006, I believe God spoke a promise to me when He said I was going to have an "amazing second half." The day I wrote that in my Journal, I had no idea what that meant or why I would need to hear those words as His promise to me.

During the next year, there were several times I revisited God's promise to me. Then, eight months later, my position, in a matter of five, short minutes, was eliminated due to budget cuts for 2008. Guess where I headed during those days of shock and transition? Back to God's promise: "Steve, you're going to have an amazing second half."

There is nothing more refreshing than to have someone tell you what they will do *and then do it*—especially when you are depending on them. Knowing we can count on someone, we call him a "man of his word." Likewise, nothing rocks a relationship with a family member, business associate, or a friend quite like a broken promise.

It's true, I still don't know all that it means, but I am hanging onto God's promise while making my way along The Journey. And today I can tell you, God is faithful!

Our Father God has given many promises in His Word. This week's personal note is focused on two very important promises. Either these promises are good, or we've got a problem. As you read the Scripture, consider what God has promised and let it impact how you will live your life.

THE FATHER'S HEART

When do you need a promise? Isn't it when you need assurance from someone as to what they will or will not do? Often you just want people to do what they say; other times, you want to know if they will follow through. Although a promise is a promise, the most valued promises don't revolve around tasks, but around relationships.

My *greatest* promises are about our relationship. My promise is about setting things right between us and doing something for you. When it comes to your relationship with Me, you must trust Me to do what I promise.

The turning point for your life comes when you understand My promise and when you trust Jesus Christ to place you in right standing with Me. Even David understood how wonderful this promise was when he wrote: "Blessed are they whose transgressions are forgiven, whose sins are covered. Blessed is the man whose sin the Lord will never count against him" (Psalm 32:1–2).

This fortunate, blessed state is what I promise you. Your response is to exercise faith in Me to deliver. Your life will change for the better once you believe what I promised you. Fulfillment of a promise depends on both of us. You must receive and believe; I must deliver. Your faith *activates* My promise. Faith releases you to live *not* on the basis of what you see you can't do, but on what I say I will do.

Abraham did not focus on his impotence; throw up his hands, and say, "It's hopeless." Rather he maintained his focus on Me and My promise. He gathered strength from his faith and gave Me glory knowing I had the power to do what I said I would do.

When it seems hopeless you are positioned for My promise. This is what I offer you as My child. Through the sacrifice of Jesus on the cross—His death for your sins—you are made right with Me. *This is My greatest promise to you.*

As you know, a promise is only as good as the one who declares it. Do you consider Me trustworthy, faithful, and able to deliver? The power of a promise depends on the reliability of the promise giver.

Let's consider another great promise I'm making you: the promise of the return of My Son. The day of judgment and the return of Christ *is* a big deal. Perhaps His return may seem slow in coming to you, but delay is not an indicator of impotence. I will deliver. The "delay" is because I don't want anyone to be lost. The longer I wait to send My Son, the more space and time people have to enter into right relationship with Me.

Uncertainty as to when Jesus will return is a means of grace. The lack of predictability regarding the end of this age is designed to help you live today with a different perspective. As you live with expectancy and eagerly anticipate the arrival of Jesus, grace flows into your life as a citizen of heaven *today*. My promise of a new heaven and a new earth is given to help you commit to My kingdom *today*. It's not to scare you, but to keep you focused *today*.

Not only do I promise you Christ's righteousness, but that Jesus Christ will put everything in order. Let this promise guide your choices today. Make every effort to live in purity and peace, imitating Jesus. Don't confuse My patient restraint regarding the day of judgment as a failure to deliver on My promise.

My child, I love you so much and want only the very best for you. That's why I give you these promises. Jesus will transform your earthly body into a glorious body just like His resurrected body. You will be made complete by My power, the same power I'll use to put everything back as it should be.

So allow these promises to keep you focused on the goal. Then you will obtain everything I have for you as you live totally committed to Me.

I love you,
Abba

YOUR HEART

In your quiet time with God, ask Him this question: "Father, what would You like to say to me today?" Write what you believe He is saying to you. Write your name, and begin to capture whatever comes to mind, just as if God were speaking to you. For you see, He is…

Now, take a moment to write your thoughts to our Father.

Here are a couple of questions to help you reflect on The Promises of God:

- What is most encouraging to you from reading this week's thoughts?

- What are some of God's promises to you? How has He fulfilled them?

- Where do you need to hear God's promise along The Journey today?

Prayer

Father, thank You for loving me and for sending Jesus to set things right between us. May the uncertainty of the end-time become grace in my daily life, and help me focus on Your purpose for my life on this earth. Help me to live with eager expectation of Jesus' return, so I pursue living my life for You. In Jesus' name, amen.

Week 16

FACE-TO-FACE

Devotional Scriptures

Genesis 3
Exodus 2:23-3:1–10
Isaiah 55
2 Corinthians 3:7–18; 4:1–19
John 1:1–18

The Psalmist's Pen

Psalm 27

FROM STEVE'S HEART

Recently, Rita went out of town for a few days. I had a full load of work during her trip, and I thought my busy schedule would help me from missing her too much. Was I wrong! I have never missed Rita more! Our phone conversations were longer and more frequent through the day, and the quality of our sleep was embarrassingly pitiful. We really enjoy being together—we've been best friends for more than thirty years.

That weekend, I was working in the yard, finishing the leaf removal and scalping the lawn. It was a beautiful, spring Saturday afternoon when it happened—the moment I had been anticipating since Tuesday—*Rita walked through the gate where I was in the backyard!* My companion, best friend, partner, my helpmate, and the one whose laugh I love to hear, whose embrace I had missed was home ... we were face-to-face! Yes, I'm thankful for cell phones and unlimited long distance plans, but there is no substitute for the personal contact provided by being together.

Can you imagine how exciting it will be when the day comes for us to see Jesus face-to-face? To see the nail scarred hands and the eyes of eternal love? I am greatly anticipating the day I gaze upon my Savior's face. But until that great moment arrives, we are to continually pursue Jesus. Through His Word and His presence, we can know Him, fellowship with Him, and become more like Him.

FROM THE FATHER'S HEART

If you and I are going to connect, you must answer the same question I posed to Adam and Eve: *Where are you?* Unfortunately the question was prompted by their willful rejection of My instructions. You know they tried to hide from Me because of their sin; they went from pure innocence and paradise to a place of fear. With their disobedience (sin), they became aware of their nakedness and shame came. They became fearful and uncomfortable in My presence. They believed the lie of Satan over the truth of My Word. They chose what they wanted to believe based upon what they wanted to do.

That one decision made it uncomfortable for them to draw near to Me. There is a significant difference between living with the "fear of the Lord" and being afraid of Me. The first means you know I love you and want what is best for you. You realize I see everything going on in your life, and you seek to live pleasing to Me. The latter is when you know your choices go against what I've taught you, yet you still choose your own way.

When you are uncomfortable with the thought of being face-to-face with Me that is an indicator your choices are moving in the wrong direction. Why do you think I asked Adam and Eve where they were? It wasn't because I couldn't find them in the garden! It was so they would realize they were hiding from Me. But their hiding could not undo the choice they had made.

Another reason people avoid being face-to-face is lack of interest and motivation. When you believe the other person has nothing to offer, do you anticipate getting together? If you already know all the answers, how motivated are you? If you're not thirsty, water is of little concern. If you're not hungry, food is less interesting.

If you and I are going to come together face-to-face, then you must have desire. How interested, thirsty, hungry, or desperate are you to discover My purpose for your life? I want you to come, pursue, learn, live, and receive from Me.

Remember, My thoughts are not like your thoughts. My ways are not your ways. See how high the sky soars above the earth? That is how far My ways surpasses your way and your thinking! But what I offer you is access to My ways and My thoughts so you can make the most of The Journey. I want you to be engaged in the process of coming together. When you come to Me, you will live in joy and experience a whole and complete life.

Like the rain, My Word is sent to produce life and help you grow. There is no need to hide from Me. No need to spend your life on stuff that will not satisfy. Seek My face. Come let us meet together; live for My purpose and glory and your joy and fulfillment.

I love you,
Abba

YOUR HEART

In your quiet time with God, ask Him this question: "Father, what would You like to say to me today?" Write what you believe He is saying to you. Write your name, and begin to capture whatever comes to mind, just as if God were speaking to you. For you see, He is ...

Now, take a moment to write your thoughts to our Father.

As you consider being face-to-face with God, here are a few questions to help reflect along The Journey:

- How important is your one-on-one time with God?

- What hinders you from being face-to-face with Him?

- What behavior may make it hard to come before God? What would you like to do about it?

- If you were to make an appointment to spend time with God, when would you schedule it? When would you like to start?

Prayer

Father, thank You for loving me enough to not leave me alone in my shame. Thank You for walking where I am in order to find me and call me out. Forgive me for hiding from You when I know right now all You want is what is best for me. Forgive me for my failure to meet You face-to-face. I am so thankful for Your continual pursuit of my heart; grant me grace to seek Your face. I love You. In Jesus' name, amen.

Week 17

GOD'S PURSUIT

Devotional Scriptures

Luke 19:1–10
Matthew 18:10–14
Ezekiel 36:22–30
Jeremiah 30:1–10
Hebrews 2:1–18
Romans 5:1–11

The Psalmist's Pen

Psalm 107

FROM STEVE'S HEART

Not long ago, Rita and I made a trip to the Kansas City area where our youngest daughter lived. Although we did some HGTV-type work on their apartment, our primary purpose was to participate in the dedication of Judah, Brian and Melanie's firstborn son, our fifth grandchild.

Infant dedication is a community-based act of worship. Parents come to the altar of the church to acknowledge their child as a gift from God and to give back the gift to God. Brian and Melanie, along with family and local church members, commit to living their lives as followers of Jesus in order to help Judah come to know Jesus Christ as Savior and Lord. It is a faith act for all where we recognize the need for God's grace through family and the body of Christ to help nurture the young.

Following the dedication service, our family gathered for lunch. It was then that Rita brought Maggie, our first granddaughter to me.

"She has something to tell you," Grandma said. In a bashful, childlike manner, she told me she asked Jesus into her heart. I gave her a hug and expressed my joy in hearing this good news. She went on to tell me her story that she prayed to receive Jesus the previous Sunday during children's church.

Five years earlier I prayed the dedication prayer with our oldest daughter Stephanie and her husband, Jeffrey when they dedicated Maggie to the Lord. Perhaps you can appreciate the joy of hearing Maggie's story on the same day her cousin Judah was dedicated. The parents' act of faith in infant dedication has to be validated by the child's personal faith when they come to an age of understanding.

The Bible tells us that the Son of Man came to *seek* and to save what was lost. It is a childlike faith that allows us to hear and respond to the story of Jesus' birth and life, His teaching and minis-try, crucifixion, burial, resurrection, and long-anticipated return.

No matter how old you are, I hope you celebrate and welcome "God's Pursuit." The Journey this week reminds us that it was God in the person of Jesus Christ that came seeking us even *before* we understood we were lost.

FROM THE FATHER'S HEART

I've been reaching out towards humanity since the Beginning. Although nature, prophets, and other leaders have testified of Me, nothing and no one so reveals Myself completely as My Son. Jesus perfectly reflects who I am so you can know Me. He is holding things together by His powerful word. Right now, following His sacrificial death for your sins, He sits at my right hand in His hon-ored place of highest rank and honor over all creation. Through His life, death, and resurrection, I offer you salvation.

Everything that Jesus has done and purchased for you was motivated by My love for you. I sought you out. There is nothing for you to add to My redemptive plan; forgiveness of your sins only requires your faith and obedience. Jesus came to you in your lost condition. I offer you freedom from the fear of death. I provided the sacrifice for your sins. It is finished. When you understand why I pursued you, you will rejoice in the hope this brings, for you stand in My presence unconditionally loved and guilt free.

You also have hope when life presses in on you. Suffering develops patience in you, patience produces perseverance, perseverance develops character, and character keeps you alert to what I'm going to do next. Instead of being defeated, you can now live with expectancy. When the world was void of hope, I sent Jesus to bring My hope to humanity. When you were too weak or rebellious to reach out to Me, I still reached out to you. With infinite love, I searched for you until I found you.

Jesus came to seek you out, demonstrating My love for you while you were still a sinner. When you were lost, I sought you out in order to set you right with Me. Now that you are in right relationship with Me, just think how I can expand your life, your purpose, and our relationship.

My child, I offer friendship to you. I love you and have only your best interest in mind. I want to fill your life with hope. All My resources are available to you so you may live well and pleasing to Me. Allow Me to fill your life with hope as you continue to seek My face.

I love you,
Abba

YOUR HEART

In your quiet time with God, ask Him this question: "Father, what would You like to say to me today?" Write what you believe He is saying to you. Write your name, and begin to capture whatever

comes to mind, just as if God were speaking to you. For you see, He is ...

Now, take a moment to write your thoughts to our Father.

Here are a couple of questions to help you reflect on God's Pursuit:

- What is most encouraging to you from reading this week's thoughts?

- When did you first notice God's pursuit of you? Recently? How did you respond?

- How does the idea of God's pursuit impact you?

- How has your relationship changed over the past six months?

Prayer

Father, Your love moves You to seek us out—first for our salvation, and then for transformation and fellowship. Thank You for the finished work of the cross. I pray that as I continue to seek You, You reveal more of Yourself to me each day. In Jesus' name, amen.

Week 18

LIFE-GIVING POWER

Devotional Scriptures

> John 17:1–19
> Romans 6:1–14
> John 10:22–30
> Matthew 16:21–28
> Luke 8:40–56
> John 12:44–50

The Psalmist's Pen

> Psalm 36

FROM STEVE'S HEART

She was only seven years old when a twelve-year-old boy took advantage of her sexually. For two years she struggled with the experience while her mother tried to figure out why her daughter was not the same girl. No longer the smiling, innocent, little girl, she was depressed and withdrawn. They're working through it.

She was raised in a Christian home, but she began to associate with the wrong crowd. At eighteen, she broke her parents' hearts by moving out and marrying a man against their advice. To this day, they are concerned about their daughter, but they are working through it.

His wife is battling cancer. She has already "won" since they only gave her five years to live—*twenty* years ago. She tells her doctor she and God are on the thirty-year plan. But the cancer has returned, and they have their eighteen-year-old granddaughter living with them. She has so much potential but is choosing to not live in pursuit of her destiny. They're working through it.

Not headlines on the news but stories shared in the course of one week.

These grievous life situations abound, and there are others even more tragic. In fact, your story might be one of the tougher situations. This week The Journey calls us to remember who has *life-giving power*. Although the enemy seeks to destroy, none of these stories are beyond the reach of God's capacity to act and grant life when those involved turn to Him for mercy and grace.

FROM THE FATHER'S HEART

One winter day, someone in the crowd asked Jesus, "How long will you keep us in suspense?" The question probed His identity and place in prophecy as the Messiah. To be doubtful, undecided, and uncertain is a choice people make regarding My Son, Jesus. He fulfilled the prophecy spoken about the Christ. Actually it's pretty easy to move from suspense to certainty—just believe the Scripture's revelation.

The accounts of Jesus' life—the miracles, His teachings, crucifixion, resurrection, and post-resurrection appearances—were witnessed by many. My Word delivers the story. Of course, those who choose not to believe receive what they believe. Remember, it is not My will that any should perish.

I want you to understand my ability and power to give life—eternal life through Jesus Christ. To all who believe, my gift is life without end. Death only moves you into My presence. I give you a place that is secure where nothing can snatch you out of My hand. Yes, The Journey includes suffering, but don't be confused about the big picture. My Son and I are one; what He accomplished was by My power and authority granted. Suspend the suspense; listen, believe and obey; My gift of life is for you.

Just before His betrayal what do you see Jesus do? Right, you find Him praying. He prays for Himself, His disciples, for you as one who through their eye witness accounts will believe. The time had come.

I placed Jesus in charge of everything, granted Him authority over all people. Why? So He could give you life—real and eternal, abundant life. And what is this "eternal life"? That you *know* Me - the one and only true God and Jesus Christ whom I sent.

To know *about* Me is *not* to know Me. Who do you know? In one sense you *know* a lot of people, but in the eternal life sense of *know* you only have a handful of people you know deeply, through exposure, and conversation, and shared experiences, right? Your knowing comes from your personal relationship with them—it's the same with Me. You see the potential of knowing demonstrated in Jesus' relationship with Me.

Eternal life is to know Me in an intimate, connected, relational way; this comes through knowing My Son, Jesus Christ. Jesus revealed My character in great detail, so you see Me in Him.

The power to give life is mine and I gave it to Jesus. As you accept His words and life sacrifice for your sins I give you eternal life. Just as My life and character was displayed in His life, His life and character are to be displayed in your life. I will protect you as you *pursue this life*—that's The Journey.

You are one who believes in Jesus, right? You accept the account of those eyewitness disciples, right? Now I want you to understand and stay aligned with My goal: that all My People be one in heart and mind. Just as I was in Jesus, and He was in Me, you may be one with Us.

Why is this so important? So the world might believe that I really did send Jesus. The message is passed on as My people are one—My life in Jesus, His life in you. When My people are one with Christ and as the Body of Christ this provides the unbelieving world evidence of My unconditional love and redemptive plan. This lets them see how much I love them and because of My love, how I sent Him to deliver the message.

People are struggling around you, hidden in the crowd like the woman with the hemorrhage for twelve long years, ashamed and living in the margins of life. Many have been taken advantage of by the systems of the world, by the one who seeks to steal, kill, and destroy. Others will come to the end of their pride only when hit by life's difficulties or a tragedy much like Jairus, the synagogue ruler. When his twelve-year-old daughter was hurting, he didn't care any longer about what others might think!

Now, look at these two life situations. Look at them in the context of *I have the power to give life.* Look at them as you think about the situations of people around you, not just as miracles.

No matter what the situation, you may rest assured I have the ability to give life. I call you to Myself through Jesus. I call you to believe, to know Me, and experience abundant life. I want you to experience My love through Jesus, to be set apart from the world by letting the truth of My Word have its way in your daily life, and I call you to embrace the mission to serve the lost people all around you who do not know Me.

The needs *are* great. As you continue to mature in knowing Me, My power to give life will not only be your experience but will flow through your life. That's The Journey.

I love you,
Abba

YOUR HEART

In your quiet time with God, ask Him this question: "Father, what would You like to say to me today?" Write what you believe He is saying to you. Write your name, and begin to capture whatever comes to mind, just as if God were speaking to you. For you see, He is …

Now, take a moment to write your thoughts to our Father.

Here are a couple of questions to help you reflect on God's life-giving power:

- How has your life been threatened?

- How did you reach out to God for help? What happened?

- Do you know someone who is struggling today? How might you reach out to them?

- What is most encouraging to you from reading this week's thoughts?

Prayer

Father, I rejoice in Christ's victory over death and therefore, my victory over sin as I am united with Him in the resurrection. Now, may the same power displayed in the resurrection be manifest in my mortal body allowing me to experience life abundantly, now and for eternity in Your presence. Amen.

RIGHT CHOICES COST

(Palm Sunday)

Devotional Scriptures

Acts 14:19–28
1 Peter 2:9–25
1 Corinthians 1:3–11
Isaiah 53:1–9
Isaiah 53:10–12
Philippians 2:1–11

The Psalmist's Pen

Psalm 56

FROM STEVE'S HEART

It was in an unfamiliar area of the city. The building was awkwardly located. Not well marked or friendly for first time visitors or perhaps it was just my apprehension. I was dressed for networking—coffee shop appointments that day, wearing a sport coat and dress shirt, no tie. This was one of my Thursday morning appointments.

It had been pretty easy to fill out the paperwork online, even the phone conversation allowed me to maintain my anonymity. But the process required me to show up and bring two forms of identity. This was the first time in over thirty years that I found myself filing for unemployment insurance and registering for employment; I was at the Workforce Oklahoma Tulsa office.

Did I mention that it was a humbling experience? My entry into the building took me by one office where a large number of people were standing in line and sitting in rows of chairs; they were in need of some assistance. I climbed the stairs to Suite 450 in search of the Employment Office.

Gail greeted me, and assured me I was in the right place and that the additional paperwork was necessary.

"They never tell you about this step," she repeated over and over to all of us who thought we were just supposed to show our photo ID. She was kind...they were under-staffed...I learned she was filling in for someone that day...she was helpful.

While observing my new peers, I couldn't help but wonder what their stories were...and did I mention that it was a humbling experience? Driving home in silence, I tried to process it; I still am.

This morning I read Philippians 2:5–11 about the incredibly humbling process Jesus experienced.

No, I cannot imagine. Yes, I can only imagine.

No, I can't it figure out. Yes, I believe it.

Here is what I received...will you ask our Father, "*What would You like to say to me today?*"

FROM THE FATHER'S HEART

When you are afraid, re-connect to your trust in Me. I am God. My Word is sure, no need to fear mortal man or spiritual opposition—I am God Almighty.

Your battle is not in human form, men attacking you in pride or twisting your words or plotting to harm you as it was for David. The attack is on your mind, your heart, your spirit. The enemy's strategies and deceit are aimed at your thoughts. Indeed, your struggle is not against people but against Satan and all his of servants—rulers, authorities, powers of this dark world, and the spiritual forces of evil in the heavenly realms.

Be prepared but not afraid. Take up each weapon I've given you.

Stand firm with truth, righteousness, peace, faith, and salvation; all provided in Jesus. Apply these realities to your life. My Word is a primary weapon and so is prayer in your ongoing warfare. Pray often about all things. Pray for others. Keep your eyes open and stay alert. Stay connected with others in order to encourage and be encouraged.

You are correct to call out for help. I am here for you. Rejoice in My Word, trust in Me, and fear not. Fulfill your vows, your commitment to Me. Cultivate a spirit of gratitude; warfare will wear you down. Heart-felt and expressed thanksgiving is revitalizing! I have rescued you from death and stabilized your stumbling steps. Now you may walk before Me in the land of the living.

An incredibly humbling process was endured by Jesus. Remember? He was God, yet did not think so much of Himself that He held tightly on to His status or advantage. No, when it was time, He became Son of Man, a slave, a human being, a servant. No special privileges. Jesus lived a self-less, obedient life and completed My purpose. Jesus died a self-less, obedient death—indeed, the worst death a man could experience: death on a cross!

The cost of a right choice has to be paid before the reward of a right choice can be received.

Because of His obedience I exalted Him high above all things in heaven and earth. I gave Him the Name that is above all names. And be certain of this: every knee, in heaven and earth will bow in worship before Him; all creation, all men will call out in praise that He is the Master of all—*Jesus Christ is Lord.*

So when afraid, check your level of trust in Me; I am God, it will be as I say. The price has been paid; it's only a matter of time. Grace and peace, my child ... grace and peace. Take heart!

I love you,
Abba

YOUR HEART

In your quiet time with God, ask Him this question: "Father, what would You like to say to me today?" Write what you believe He is saying to you. Write your name, and begin to capture whatever comes to mind, just as if God were speaking to you. For you see, He is ...

Now, take a moment to write your thoughts to our Father.

Here are a couple of questions to help you reflect on the cost of right choices:

- What do you do when your world is shaken by something unexpected?

- How is the enemy attacking your thoughts these days?

- What do you face today that may require a sacrifice on your part?

Prayer

Heavenly Father, Jesus demonstrated the character to make right choices regardless of the cost. Help me keep my eyes on Him; He is the Faithful One so I may be the same ... no matter what. I know You are faithful. Even when it seems like life is out of control and I am afraid, I will trust in You. In the Name of our Servant Lord and Savior, Jesus, amen.

THE LIVING CHRIST

(Easter Sunday)

Devotional Scriptures

Acts 3:11–16
Acts 4:1–12
Acts 5:17–32
Acts 2:22–36
Ephesians 1:15–23
2 Corinthians 4:7–18
John 20:1–18
1 Corinthians 15:19–26

The Psalmist's Pen

Psalm 23

FROM STEVE'S HEART

As they say the one constant is change. The Journey is filled with both opportunities and stretching times that can challenge our peace, joy, and rest. Suffice it to say I understand this principle.

It was a surprise turned into delight when The Journey took me to the Twenty-third Psalm. Too many of those *opportunities* had shifted to *my responsibility* and with that, the stress of *non-required-burden-bearing*. You know what I mean?

That's why I believe God spoke to me out of Psalm 23.

Steve, I am your Shepherd, let me provide all you need.

Rest in My provision and care; trust Me as I allow you to catch your breath before sending you each day in the right direction. Even when it's a tough path, the darkest valley, you need not fear as you follow Me, for I'm also by your side.

Receive security from My skilled ability to guide you, even through difficult terrain. In moments of weariness come to My table; I serve a full table—right in front of the enemy. And by My Spirit, I anoint your wounded, tempted, and weary heart until your cup overflows with My blessing.

Son, I am chasing after you every day. Why? To bestow My goodness and love on you every step of The Journey until you are home. Hear Me—this is how you will enjoy the amazing second half we're going to have; I'm your Shepherd. I am God, your Shepherd.

Watch this week.

Allow Me to provide *all* you need ...

It started that Monday morning and continued through the week; Friday morning I could identify at least fifteen incidents of significance where my Shepherd made things happen. He provided direction, made connections, gave ideas, arranged schedules, set appointments, and helped me get things done—things that were concerns and opportunities; things that had become stressful ... until I heard Him speak to me as my Shepherd.

"Watch this week," He said; yes, it has been amazing! This week I let him be my Shepherd. What a difference! The living Christ is the resurrected Jesus. He wants to be actively engaged in The Journey—yes, *your* journey.

Will you ask God, our Father: *"What would You like to say to me today?"*

FROM THE FATHER'S HEART

The Journey is about your life, your experience, your purpose, path, and destiny. It is about your understanding of My ways; working through the undeniable reality of being a physical, mental, emotional, and spiritual being. The Journey is about connecting the dots in life. Some choose to come up with their own explanations. You desire Truth, you desire Life, and you want to understand; that is My gift, too.

The Journey is about coming to understand My plan and then living it out. What an adventure! Your journey is really no different than that of anyone else in that sense. Circumstances, your place in history, and your life experiences—yes, they're unique. But in the big picture, everyone has to decide to accept My revelation, My Son, and My explanation, whether they believe or not.

The Journey is about understanding My Word. For example, even though Jesus taught and explained My plan to His disciples, they did not understand it from the Scriptures that He would raise again from the dead.

On that original resurrection morning, Mary showed up at the tomb looking for the dead body of Jesus. John and Peter came as a result of her panicked request urging them on because someone had "taken away the Master from the tomb," still not putting the pieces together. As John saw evidence in the tomb, he believed. Moments later, Mary encountered Jesus alive; she believed.

This was and is the turning point on The Journey. Without the *living* Christ you're on your own. No need to try to make sense of your purpose, struggles or any of that stuff that Satan wants to use to derail your thinking. My Word revives your daily experience of life and relationships and people; it leads you to understand your purpose, gives you hope and My peace.

For The Journey to make sense, receive the entire Message––only then can you stand firm. Jesus is the Christ, the Messiah––He died for your sins, just as Scripture declares. He was buried and raised from death on the third day, just as Scripture says; He appeared alive to Peter, John, and Mary, and later to more than 500 of His followers in one place, just as Scripture says.

Jesus, the living Christ is with you on The Journey; active, alive, involved, giving life and hope. If Christ has not been raised, then all you're doing is wandering around in the dark as lost as ever; just like everyone else with their hand-made gods. Your faith is useless without the living Christ; you're on your own in a hostile environment.

But that is not the case; I raised Him from the dead.

So, remember: the resurrection means you're not alone or ill equipped for The Journey. My Son, the living Christ, is with you as your Shepherd. *Your* Shepherd … you're not alone.

You may have a spirit of wisdom and revelation that makes you intelligent and discerning in knowing the Truth. I want you to see what I'm calling you to be and to grasp this incredible life as one who believes in Jesus, the resurrected Savior.

This power is available to you for The Journey, My strength exerted on your behalf. By the way, this demonstration of power allows you to live as My child; it is the same might I exerted to raise Jesus from the dead. Think about that! It is available so you will live as My child.

I love you,
Abba

YOUR HEART

In your quiet time with God, ask Him this question: "Father, what would You like to say to me today?" Write what you believe He is saying to you. Write your name, and begin to capture whatever comes to mind, just as if God were speaking to you. For you see, He is …

Now, take a moment to write your thoughts to our Father.

Here are a couple of questions to help you reflect on The Christ Who Lives:

- What are your thoughts about having Jesus as your Shepherd?

- How might that impact your daily experience of life that can include worry, fear, stress, discouragement, frustration, disappointment...?

- How real is the resurrection of Jesus to you? What difference does it make, really?

Prayer

Father, I confess my tendency to operate as if it all depends on me—my strength, my power, and I too often want my way...forgive me. Send me out into this day and my assignments with a consciousness of Your role as my Shepherd and my place as Your sheep. Release Your power in my life so I live victoriously over sin and self...pleasing to You in everything. Amen.

Week 21

IN CHRIST ALONE

Devotional Scriptures

Romans 6:1–23
Ephesians 2:1–10
Galatians 2:11–21
John 17:1–5
Romans 8:18–30
Revelation 1:4–8

The Psalmist's Pen

Psalm 126

FROM STEVE'S HEART

As a young person I was pretty good, but not real good, at knowing and communicating the rules of the church—the things we were known for not doing. The impact on my faith in Jesus Christ's death, burial, and resurrection as my Savior was not so much impacted...but my ability to embrace Christians whose lives did not line up with my list of socially acceptable Christian behaviors was hindered. That was a problem.

To this day, I still fumble a bit with extending grace to those who confess faith in Christ but exhibit social behaviors I grew up believing were not appropriate. Frankly, some of the stuff we pride ourselves in not doing slipped into stuff we wanted others to see, so they would know we were "good Christians." Would that be *self-righteousness?* While there was good reasoning behind the prohibitions, some were based upon culture, tradition, or how we were raised rather than biblical instruction. I don't blame anyone; it's just the way it was.

That was then; this is now. By God's grace I understand that when Jesus gave His life on the cross and said, "It is finished," all that remained was my response. I believe He died for my sins. There is nothing to be added except our faith.

Jesus was granted authority over all people so He might give eternal life to all. Eternal life is to know the Father and His Son, Jesus, whom He sent. The good news is that God's gift has no connection to rule keeping or religion—it is life in Christ. It is our personal faith in Jesus that gives us life, followed by transformation into His likeness—The Journey. God's motive in all of this is His love-driven desire for us to have life … freedom … relationship!

Will you ask God, our Father: "*What would You like to say to me today?*"

FROM THE FATHER'S HEART

There is a great place of freedom along The Journey. Once you understand you cannot be set right with Me by rule keeping or self-improvement efforts, you're on the way. When you quit trying to be good enough and understand it is only by trusting in Jesus as Messiah and your personal faith in Him, you're nearing the place of freedom. Once you quit trying to be right, you become right. In Christ you have discovered true freedom.

Freedom comes when you identify yourself completely with Christ; that takes you to the cross. To be crucified with Christ is to place yourself on the cross. This frees you from trying to appear good to others or Me and allows Christ to live in you. The life you live is then lived by faith in Jesus who loved you and gave Himself up for you. Freedom is not found in the old rule-keeping, peer-pleasing religion. Grace means you receive My free gift of a personal relationship with Me. You are set right with Me through your faith in Jesus. This is the place of freedom—the cross! Think about it. If being restored in a personal relationship with Me could have been accomplished by rules and self-mastery, then Jesus Christ died on the cross for nothing. Right?

The Journey is about making sense of and making the most out of your life. It's pretty straight forward when you think about it. The problem is so many people don't think clearly, they fail to step back and look at the way things are.

Sin is your willful, intentional disobedience to the boundaries I set for your benefit as Creator God. Of course, it is pretty easy to see this in the garden with Adam and Eve. The reality is you like to call the shots and do what is most pleasing to self, your flesh; original sin was that willful act of disobedience to My specific instruction.

There is only one God, and I am the one true God. If you want to be god of your life, that is an option, your choice, but it is not the path to freedom. There are reasons for the limits I set the commandments I put into play. Sin happens when you exercise your will over My will and intentionally do what you like. Of course, with the choice comes consequence.

The idea that living in sin is freedom is an illusion—sin leads to death and slavery; live a life of sin and your reward is death. How is that for a pension plan? Compare that plan to My gift of life—eternal life delivered, pre-paid by Jesus Christ, My Son.

The Journey is about your life path. Your choice: a stagnant life of sin leads to death, the crucified life of obedience leads to an abundant life—freedom.

Here's what's crazy: how often you allow the world—which doesn't know the first thing about living—to tell you how to live. It's the common path of man in the age-old battle. Man thinks he is living in freedom as he gratifies the cravings of his sinful nature, while following its desires and thoughts leading to slavery, not freedom. Life and freedom are found only in Christ. And Christ's life will make a difference in your daily life experience.

I love you,
Abba

YOUR HEART

In your quiet time with God, ask Him this question: "Father, what would You like to say to me today?" Write what you believe He is saying to you. Write your name, and begin to capture whatever comes to mind, just as if God were speaking to you. For you see, He is…

Now, take a moment to write your thoughts to our Father.

Here are a few questions to help you as you reflect on living in Christ alone:

- How real is Jesus Christ to you on a daily basis? Through-out your day?

- Where do you need to tap into the power of Christ instead of trying to change in your own strength?

- How important is tapping into the "Body of Christ" to your growth? What does Scripture teach about that connection?

- How is your life being shaped by the world? What do you want to do about it?

Prayer

Father, I confess my tendency to fall back into the old power play of self-government or self-righteousness. Jesus called Lazarus from the tomb and presented him alive to live again. You called Jesus from the tomb to sit at your right hand interceding in my behalf at this very moment. You have called me out from death to life, keep me free as I take up my cross today to follow Jesus, knowing it is His life that gives me life today and for eternity. Amen.

Week 22

THE UNSEEN COMPANION

Devotional Scriptures

Ezekiel 36:22–36
Genesis 17:1–8
Genesis 39:19–23
Philippians 4:1–9
Colossians 2:6–15
Acts 4:23–37

The Psalmist's Pen

Psalm 121

FROM STEVE'S HEART

Most children are pretty good in early childhood with their imagination. One of the values of reading is the ability to go places and imagine things otherwise not seen. Perhaps you were one of those children that had an imaginary friend—you talked to him or her while playing; your friend accompanied you wherever and whenever you wanted them to.

Companionship is derived from a Vulgar Latin compound combining "together" + "bread." You would have "bread together with"––a companion. The word history of *lord* is quite interesting, too. The actual, as well as the symbolic importance of bread as a basic foodstuff is exhibited by this word. *Lord* is derived from a compound formed in very early Old English times "bread" + "guardian." *Lord*, therefore, literally means "guardian of the bread." Such a position would be the dominant one in a household, so *lord* came to denote a man of authority and rank in society at large.

God, our Father has given us His Spirit so we can experience the companionship of our living Lord and Savior, Jesus Christ. Jesus, "the bread of life" desires to break bread together with us. He wants to provide you and me *companionship* for The Journey. The Father draws us to Himself through Jesus. How often do we miss the table talk, the picnic, the meal with our Lord? This One who is well established as the "Guardian of the bread" desires to protect and provide—to provide leadership and demonstrate authority for our well-being as the *Lord* of our lives.

One of the things about our imaginary childhood friends, we could control them; they accompanied us whenever we wanted or needed company. How easy to treat Jesus Christ, our Friend, like an imaginary friend; but what a loss if we do.

Are you enjoying His company? The living Lord longs to be our Companion and yes, the Guardian of our lives.

FROM THE FATHER'S HEART

So, how will you influence others for My kingdom? How will they be prepared for My Son's coming? How might you live in the real world of people where differences of opinion and interpersonal relationships can create conflict and disappointment? How do you stay on track and avoid taking offense to another person so that you don't hold a grudge against them?

Let Me be your Companion every moment of every day. Look, I'm committed to you. My delight comes from coming alongside you, to help you, to accompany you every moment of every day— your Body Guard, your Friend. I don't "know people in high places." I am the One who is that One ... you've got connections. Wherever you go, today, tomorrow, and forever, I will be there. You could not hire someone with My authority, My power, My connections, My availability—twenty-four-seven—you could not afford a personal companion like Me to guard your life. Lift up your eyes beyond the mountains, look unto Me; your strength comes from Me for I made the heavens and earth and those mountains. I am your Guardian and will not let you stumble. I am your Protection, right beside you shielding you all day long. I am guarding your path to keep you from evil—watching over your life when you go and when you come, now and forevermore.

So, back to the question—how can you be a player in your world for My kingdom and enjoy The Journey?

Rejoice. Celebrate. Be amazed with all this, with Me; rejoice in the Lord Jesus Christ all day. Knowing the reality of My love, My grace, and My commitment to you, what My companionship means for your life. I'm no imaginary friend, My friend. Let Me be real to you every moment of every day. Ask Me to remind you that I'm here, and I'll do it.

What happens when you do? You will be released from competing with others allowing you to be committed to them instead. Others will experience you in their lives as someone on their side, working with them and not against them.

Why is this important? Jesus could show up soon, and I want those you have influence on to be ready. So, rejoice in Me. Then, don't let the stuff that creates conflict between you and others or within yourself get the best of you—that stressed out feeling. How? Learn to constantly give Me what gets to you, what causes you stress, or anxiety. Give it to Me as your Lord, Companion, and Guardian. What's a Friend like Me for, if not for this?

Go ahead; give Me those concerns as they come up in your day. Why? You will receive My peace at that moment. Instead of fretting and stressing, which brings the worst out of your behavior and capabilities, My grace will go to work bringing out the best in you. You will be healthy and whole. Wisdom will allow you to see the situation from My perspective, and you won't get so worked up. It is just

My gift of bread (life) to you. When you enjoy My companionship, worry is displaced by Jesus as Lord of your life, which is wonderful and amazing, but not too good to be true.

So to help you get there and to increase your receptivity to My companionship, I want you to think. Fill your mind and think about whatever is true, noble, reputable, authentic, compelling, gracious—the best, not the worst—the beautiful, not the ugly, what is excellent and praiseworthy, not negative.

Make a habit of this type of thinking, and embrace My companionship so you will enjoy My peace. Shepherd, Guardian, Companion, Lord—that's who I want to be to you.

Enjoy The Journey, and let's make a difference today...

I love you,
Abba

YOUR HEART

In your quiet time with God, ask Him this question: "Father, what would You like to say to me today?" Write what you believe He is saying to you. Write your name, and begin to capture whatever comes to mind, just as if God were speaking to you. For you see, He is...

Now, take a moment to write your thoughts to our Father.

Here are a few questions to help you as you reflect upon companionship:

- How do you remember Jesus is with you all along?

- What could you do to practice His presence?

- How confident are you that God takes delight in you? Is that important? Why or why not?

- How do you know He takes delight in you?

Prayer

Father, I confess it is too easy for me to have a relationship of convenience with You; please forgive me. It is amazing to think You would be my companion every day. That You would give me peace as I learn to release to You what's getting to me. Help me remember You are my Companion—remind me throughout this day. And help me be aware of what I'm thinking so that I think about the right stuff. I'm so excited to know You are the Guardian of my life. Thank you! Amen.

Week 23

THE SHEPHERD

Devotional Scriptures

Jeremiah 23:1–8, 31:10–14
Ezekiel 11:14–21
John 10:1–18
1 Peter 4:1–8, 5:1–11
Revelation 7:9–17

The Psalmist's Pen

Psalm 80

FROM STEVE'S HEART

A few years ago, Rita and I enjoyed the Gospel Music Awards Music Week and Dove Awards in Nashville. The experience provided an extensive exposure to today's Christian artists and the music industry. Of course, I was out of my environment for a full week. The days started early and were full of seminars, lunches, and late evening concerts. Despite being sleep deprived and thrown into a whirlwind of activities, it was an unforgettable experience.

When we returned home from our trip, we discovered another interruption—a delayed home repair. The installation of our new wood floors was going to take two more weeks to finish. The contractor assured us it was just one of those weird things that occasionally happen when the finish coat doesn't dry right. Everything in our house was out of place—my home study was gone, my books were packed away upstairs, my study was in the kitchen with the piano. The whole house was in chaos, and my routine completely disrupted. No matter how much I love the adventure of life, I function better with my routine!

On top of these *minor details,* there were a lot of things going on in my work, and a few things with our growing family. It probably looked like your world at times, but just with different details. And all these disturbances were taking me away from my personal quiet time. Surprisingly, it's often the hectic pace of life and not tragic circumstances that derail us from our quiet time. In trying to balance the crazy speed of life, our time with the Lord ends up being the first dropped ball.

I don't know about you, but when I miss my quiet times with the Lord, the *stuff* gets bigger than God Almighty. The burden of ownership is shifted onto my shoulders as I wrestle it away from the Father's hands. And with ownership comes stress instead of His peace. My thoughts will drag me away from the shelter of the Almighty. Instead of lying down in green pastures, I run down a dusty trail. Instead of resting beside still waters, I feel parched.

There is a lot of stuff going on in our world: tragic headlines of crime, politics, wars, and rumors of war, financial pressure, everyday stuff not going as planned, health issues, human relationship stress, and bodies pushed to exhaustion with too much self-absorption. So I am not so amazed as The Journey redirects us to think of our Shepherd again.

Scripture teaches us that Jesus is the Shepherd of the sheep. Not only is He a shepherd; He is the True Shepherd. If you look up the definition of *shepherd,* it means one who herds and tends sheep; one, as a minister or teacher, who cares for and guides a group of people. The word *true* means genuine, reliable, faithful, loyal; quick and exact in sensing and responding.

The Shepherd, in His tender care, is fully responsible for the guidance and protection of the sheep. As sheep, we often want to take on the role of the Shepherd. We want to rise up on our back legs, pick up a big stick, and start trying to lead ourselves. Other times, we get so focused on the here and now, that we lose sight of our Shepherd and where He is leading us. It's so easy to keep our heads down and nibble along the sweet green grass, straying from the fold. Eventually, we find ourselves lost and disconnected from our Shepherd's care.

When we find ourselves in that place of disconnectedness, we begin to lift up a cry for help. The ever true and faithful Shepherd always comes to find us and bring us back within the safety of the flock. But if we had stayed in close proximity with Him in the first place, we wouldn't have gone through that unnecessary and exhausting experience!

Today, I would like to challenge you to stay close to the Shepherd. Despite your crammed schedule, the immediate needs of your family, or the demands of your job, take time to listen to the Shepherd. Don't try to figure out life by yourself, and don't allow the hectic pace of life to beckon you from the safety of the Shepherd's guidance. Keep your eyes on Him, and He will take care of you.

FROM THE FATHER'S HEART

Jesus is your reliable Shepherd, quick to sense and respond to your needs as His sheep. As your Shepherd, He will care for and guide you personally. Learn to know and distinguish His voice from all other voices and follow His lead.

The True Shepherd will care for you as you come to Him. You have a freedom to come and go, to enjoy provision, and to have abundant life. But there is a thief who only comes to steal, kill, and destroy. He uses deception to lead sheep astray. A true shepherd puts his life on the line for his sheep. False shepherds put the lives of the sheep on the line for their benefit. Jesus laid down His life for you. Will you follow Him as the Shepherd of your life?

This is just another picture for you to see My heart. To see

Jesus is to see Me. To understand this Shepherd/sheep analogy is to understand the depth of My commitment to you and your well-being. Many voices call your name, but learn to discern the True Shepherd's voice. Hear Me calling, and train your ear with My Word.

Have you noticed the impact of running hard a whole week with limited rest—without the Shepherd's care? Slow down and breathe. Allow Me to provide for you.

Remember, Jesus went through everything you're going through and more (except sin); *learn to think like Him.* Think of suffering as My way of weaning you from that old, sinful habit of expecting to get your own way. That will allow you to live The Journey in pursuit of what I want for you, not what you want *or* what someone else wants for you. If you follow Me, you will experience freedom. If you choose not to follow Me, your life will become entangled in the pursuit of only what you want. Just walk with Me by faith like Abraham did—this life is one of going without knowing.

Stay alert, clear-minded, and self-controlled. Listen to Me, so we connect. Love others knowing that love covers and makes up for practically anything. Trust Me; I am your Shepherd. When your life is difficult because you're doing what I've told you to do, rejoice and trust Me. I know what I'm doing, and there's nothing that man can do to stop Me from leading you into green pastures and beside cool waters.

Work with others, and be an example; show them what it looks like to be My person. Walk in humility, especially in times of suffering. Be real by making a Jesus-response your reality, and don't react as the world would or with a self-centered reaction.

I take delight in humble, plain, ordinary, teachable sheep. Humble yourself and be content with who you are. Embrace how I created you, and then you will be able to come alongside others instead of competing with them. Simply, be like Jesus.

My strong, loving Shepherd-hand is on your life. I will do the promoting, the placement. I will order your steps and grant you favor. I will lift you up at just the right time and place. When you know Me as Shepherd, you will experience freedom to walk like Abraham and journey like Jesus. You will be carefree as you travel through life as My sheep. When you cast all your anxiety on Me and let Me be your True Shepherd, your life will be full of peace.

Enjoy The Journey and let Me, the True Shepherd, lead you today.

I love you,
Abba

YOUR HEART

In your quiet time with God, ask Him this question: "Father, what would You like to say to me today?" Write what you believe He is saying to you. Write your name, and begin to capture whatever comes to mind, just as if God were speaking to you. For you see, He is ...

Now, take a moment to write your thoughts to our Father.

Here are a couple of questions to help you reflect on walking with The Shepherd:

- What speaks to you from reading this week's thoughts?

- How consistently are you spending time with God for the purpose of building your relationship? If you desire more time, what could you do to let that happen?

- What do you do when you make a decision? How do you seek the Lord's counsel?

- What distractions seek to pull you away from following the Shepherd? Can anything be done about them?

Prayer

Shepherd of my life, I praise Your Name! You are my True Shepherd, trustworthy, faithful, loving, and merciful. We are just the sheep of Your hand, and I need You to lead me. Forgive me for not listening and for running hard on my own. Grant me grace so Your voice is the one I hear over all the others and the one I obey to the glory of Your name. Amen.

LIVING CLOSE TO GOD

Devotional Scriptures

Psalm 18:1–29
Matthew 7:21–28
Mark 12:28–34
James 1:19–26
Colossians 1:15–29
Ephesians 3:14–21

The Psalmist's Pen

Psalm 34

FROM STEVE'S HEART

The difference is huge, not in spelling but the pronunciation. Did I mean *close* [*klos*] or *close* [*kloz*]? Our language is amazing. Did you mean: near in relationship *or* to shut or bring to an end? It depends on how you say it, not how you spell it.

We all know life isn't fair and stuff happens. Sometimes it seems pretty random, but more often it comes as a consequence of our own choices, right? So when stuff happens, we have a choice—we can close God out or stay close to God. It all depends on how you live it, not just how you say it.

No, it's not easy to discern what is going on when you are in the midst of the battle during the difficult, waiting room times. That's why wisdom is so critical. We must gain the ability to see life from God's perspective, or we will be blown all over the place without His peace. The fog of war makes it hard to see. But then again, this is a faith adventure. The Journey calls us to *stay close to God* lest we unintentionally close God out.

But lest we forget, the battle between self-rule and God-rule reoccurs through the seasons of life. Why would someone close God out? One reason may be we want to be god and we're afraid God may not let us have our way or call the shots? Why do people close people out? Isn't it because something gets between them and closes off the closeness? Our relationships, with God or others are damaged when we take offense. Quite often, whether with God or other people, the offense is over unfulfilled expectations.

What's going on in your world? Are you closing God out or staying close to Him? How are your relationships? Have you received God's grace to forgive the offense, or is it destroying the closeness once experienced? Staying close to God requires faith, faith to stand on the firm foundation of the Gospel and keep a firm grip on the Shepherd's hand. When we come close to God we are impacted by His love. As we understand His love, we can think and make wiser choices along The Journey.

As you pursue closeness to God ask Him: *"What would You like to say to me today?"*

FROM THE FATHER'S HEART

In your distress, during your difficult season, cry out to Me; I will respond. The enemy is too strong for you to handle on your own, harassing you day and night. But I am here in support, even when you do not recognize Me. I am bringing you out into a spacious place.

Every time you're in the thick of it—in the battle for your life, distressed, confused, fearful, hurt, or attacked—cry out to Me. The enemy is going to attack—that goes with the human experience, even Jesus got that. The Journey teaches you to cry out to Me. *In your distress, call to Me for help* … that is not a problem.

As you cry out, know that your cries reach Me—I hear you. Know that before you see the evidence, things are being shaken at My movement toward you, as I come to your side. Know that I respond to the sound of your cry in My ear. Know that the deep waters will not overtake you as you cry out to Me. My purpose will be fulfilled—victorious over the enemies' resistance, even direct attacks. Know that I, the Lord God Almighty, I am your strength and support until your moment of breakthrough.

Know that there is a spacious place I am bringing you out to. There you will gain freedom to fully become who you are in Christ. There you will come out from the pressure of the season more fully developed as My child (mature). You are uniquely you … filled with My Spirit moving you to your destiny, transformation into the likeness of Jesus while living in the present.

Know that the place of breakthrough is broad; although clearly defined, it lacks precise limits. It is your place, open space, a spacious place, a broad path to walk out your journey. Yes, I know this is amazing, but it is true. This spacious place allows Me to interact with all of your choices, your talents, your interests, your individuality, your circumstances, your journey. It's a place with definite but indefinite boundaries—a spacious place.

Your spacious place allows you freedom to develop and explore and contribute to My kingdom in your own unique way, having passed through the place of distress. Your spacious place is defined by incredible possibilities to the glory of My name.

The desires of our hearts and the realities of your humanity meet there. What appeared to be a certain defeat becomes an amazing triumph. Yes, much like the death *and* resurrection of Jesus!

Do you see why I want you to stay close to Me? Turn to Me now in your season of testing. Know that this path leads to your transformation; the spacious place will appear before you, season after season along The Journey—following failure, following obedience, following an attack, following a victory.

You'll have to think about this one, but remember, how you are is how you will see Me. That's why you are tempted to close me out. Learn to see Me and know Me as I am, not as you are. Seek Me through My Word and the means of grace offered you through the body of Christ. With My help you are victorious.

Remember to look at Jesus, and you will see Me, the God who cannot be seen. Look at Jesus, and when you *get it,* you will understand My purpose in all things created. You will discover your purpose as well. Everything comes together, is fixed, and fits together, because of His blood poured down from the cross.

Think about it. Your life changed from rebellious, alienated, with wrong thinking, leading to misguided behavior. Now you are reconciled—brought over to My side and a whole and holy life in My sight. How did that happen? Jesus gave Himself at the cross, actually dying for you, so you could be close to Me. Remember, staying close to Me keeps you from walking away from My gift.

How do you stay close to Me? Remain grounded and steady in a connected trust. Hold on to the Message, the Gospel so you are not distracted or diverted.

Stay close to Me, remain in faith and trust; wait, hold on, and know I will be there. Stay close to Me, bound by oneness of purpose, shared heart desires, and common interests. Demonstrate loyalty and love as you are loved. Stay close to Me, don't shut me out in the difficult seasons and try to go it alone; seek My face, exercise your faith and trust Me—then you will receive My peace.

Keep your door open and we will take The Journey together. You will be amazed through it all as you figure out the depth of My love for you. Stay close to Me, and I will work with, and in, and through you by My Spirit to do more than you could ever imagine, guess, request, or dream of. Stay close to Me, and you will be transformed; people will see Jesus in you like you see Me in Jesus.

Enjoy The Journey; as you stay close to Me, I will lead you ...

I love you,
Abba

YOUR HEART

In your quiet time with God, ask Him this question: "Father, what would You like to say to me today?" Write what you believe He is saying to you. Write your name, and begin to capture whatever comes to mind, just as if God were speaking to you. For you see, He is ...

Now, take a moment to write your thoughts to our Father.

Here are a couple of questions to help you reflect on Living Close to God:

- Have you ever closed God out? What pushed you away from staying close to Him?

- What do you hear when reading this week's thoughts?

- What does it mean to "cry out to God"? Are you ...?

- How deeply do you trust God? How do you know?

Prayer

Father, my desire is to stay close to You—to never close You out of my daily life experience. Grace me to be quick to listen, slow to speak and slow to be angry; may I live the righteous life You expect of me. I rejoice in Your invitation to cry out to You in the midst of the stuff. I rejoice in Your promise to bring me out into my unique, spacious place. I stand amazed. Thank You! Help me to be sensitive to those around me who may need an encouraging word on the way to their spacious place ... I love You. In Jesus' name I pray, amen.

Week 25

LOVING OTHERS

Devotional Scriptures

Romans 12:9–21
Colossians 3:12–17
Galatians 5:1–15
1 John 2:7–17; 3:1–18; 4:7–21
John 14:23–29

The Psalmist's Pen

Psalm 128

FROM STEVE'S HEART

In his song, "What the World Needs Now," Hal David captured man's innate desire and search for lasting love:

What the world needs now is love, sweet love
It's the only thing that there's just too little of
What the world needs now is love, sweet love,
No not just for some but for everyone.

Lord, we don't need another mountain,
There are mountains and hillsides enough to climb
There are oceans and rivers enough to cross,
Enough to last till the end of time.

Original lyrics by Hal David, music composed by Burt Bacharach

This song is an artistic echo of man's life long journey to find love and fulfillment. Although love is a core need of every human, there are a myriad of attitudes, behaviors, prejudices, and stigmas that separate human beings from loving one another. My sense is that Hal David and all those who have sung his song—Burt Bacharach, the Carpenters, Jack DeShannon, or even the finalists of American Idol Season Two—were trying to start a *spiritual* renewal. They were endeavoring to convey a truth and to motivate people to fulfill the missing element of love. But because the world doesn't have a true vision of real love, they aren't able to offer a true solution to the problem.

Scripture does indicate that this world is bankrupt in love. The Bible also gives a clear definition of love and the only way to fill the aching void in the human heart. John 3:16 tells us that God so *loved the world* (that's plenty of love for all of us!) that He gave His Son to demonstrate His love for all of us by laying down His life on the cross.

Love is countless in the number of people it affects and varied in the depth of its intensity. The term *love* itself carries multiple definitions: a feeling of kindness or brotherhood toward others; an intense affection for another person based on personal or family ties; a strong affection for or attachment to another person based on regard or shared experiences or interests; an intense attraction to another person based mainly on sexual desire; and God's mercy and benevolence toward humans.

Love is never alone in its quest. It always seeks another person or object to satisfy its affection. The word *another* can mean one more; one of an undetermined number or group. By its very nature, love cannot be fulfilled until it finds a recipient of its heart.

The Journey calls us to release the *abundance of God's love* to the "just too little of" in our world. We are further reminded how His high calling requires more than feelings, but significant grace and our ability to make choices.

As you pursue being an obedient follower of Jesus, ask our Father: *"What would You like to say to me today?"*

FROM THE FATHER'S HEART

Let's begin with this truth—*loving Me includes loving people.*

Let Me show you what that looks like. Most people mistakenly base love on *feelings.* While there are certain feelings that come with love, true love is more than just a sense of warmth, attraction, or affection for another person. "Feeling-love" may include an intense affection for another person who is like family. Feeling-love may also be derived from shared life experiences or interests or a regard for another person. Feeling-love may also define that intense attraction between a man and a woman accompanied by sexual desire expressed within the boundary of marriage. Feeling-love can even manifest as kindness or brotherhood. But real love—My love—is more than all of this.

The love I want expressed comes from the core of who you are in Christ. It is beyond feeling-love. This is more than you can muster up on your own; it's more than natural human love. It is a self-giving, personal commitment to others irrespective of whether they give a grateful response or not; it is directed by your will (not emotions) and is empowered by My grace. It is divine love. This is about your *will* to love, not merely an emotional, feeling-based, natural inclination towards others.

To love one another means you want what is best for others. You seek their highest good. You extend unselfish, outgoing affection and tenderness for others—*all others*—without necessarily expecting anything in return. It is an issue of the heart and will as you choose to love even if you do not feel like loving. This love is far from anything natural; it is a supernatural love flowing from My heart into yours.

Loving from the heart without hypocrisy cannot be faked. This is not "I love you because …" This is "I choose to love you wanting what is best for you, regardless of your response." One is easy; the other requires grace. This is who I am.

You understand it wasn't because you loved Me that Jesus came and died on the cross to restore our relationship—it was totally driven by My love for you. Because I put you in right standing with Myself, I have made you able to love like this. I am love and My love is *released through you* as a result of your relationship with Me.

Don't you think I would expect the same quality of love to flow out of My People that I give? It's My life in you that makes this self-less love even a possibility. If you want to know the quality of your spiritual life—the maturity level of your faith—then do this: examine how you love others in your world. Again, this is not the feeling-love but "Jesus-love," which originates with your will and is selfless, seeking the best interest of others. That love is visible in Jesus—He chose the cross even though He was totally innocent rejected, denied, deserted, humiliated, and spat upon. That is My love.

When you confess Jesus as My Son and your Savior, you enter into an intimate relationship with Me. Having experienced *firsthand* My love and forgiveness, you are positioned to extend My love to others.

I am Love. To live in Me and to have My life in you is to live a life of love. To know Me and to live out your life extending My love is not only the expectation but provides you confidence regarding the future. There is no fear here—not because of an adolescent, uninformed view of life, but because of a mature outlook and understanding of love.

First, you were loved *before* you loved Me. Now, you love others in the same way. If you think that you can love God while hating others, your thinking is amiss. How can you say you love Me, the God you cannot see, if you won't love the person right in front of you—the person in your home, in your family, at work, across the street, with different skin color?

Loving Me includes loving people.

If you claim to be intimate with Me, you ought to live the same kind of life Jesus lived. If you claim to live in My light, but still hate another person, then you are walking in darkness. The only way to stay in the light and *not block the light from others* is to love—not with feeling-love only, but with divine love.

Consider what this looks like in your relationships. Start by looking at those who have offended you. Do you have feelings of hostility or a strong dislike for that person? Are you withholding common courtesy, a generous response of grace and forgiveness, or a genuine desire for the best for others? If you are, that is hate. Failure to forgive is the first indicator of hate and a failure to relate with divine love.

Practically everything that goes on in the world involves wanting—wanting your own way, wanting everything for yourself, wanting to appear important. All self-centered wanting has nothing to do with Me. In fact, it *isolates* you from Me. The wanting world, the all-about-me-world is on the way out. Do what I command, and you are set for eternity.

You have been chosen for this life of love. The greatest thing you can *put on* is love. It unifies and makes you whole. Don't let feelings mold your life, but rather let My Word and love shape the very essence of who you are and who you will become.

The Journey will give you ample opportunity to learn and practice loving one another; stay close to Me, and I will grant you grace to love others as I love you.

I love you,
Abba

YOUR HEART

In your quiet time with God, ask Him this question: "Father, what would You like to say to me today?" Write what you believe He is saying to you. Write your name, and begin to capture whatever comes to mind, just as if God were speaking to you. For you see, He is …

Now, take a moment to write your thoughts to our Father.

Here are a few suggestions to help you reflect on loving others:

- How does your experience of God's love influence your ability to love others?

- What does it take for us to love others?

- Who may need your love today? How will you demonstrate your love for that person?

Prayer

Father, I am seeing You are love. Fill me afresh with Your love, so I will love as You love. Forgive me for allowing the love of the world to squeeze out my love for You and hinder the release of Your love through me. Grant me grace to die to self, to live in love, and to walk in the light of Your Word... free to give, to live, to love. May others experience Your unconditional love through their association with me to the glory of Your name. Amen.

Week 26

ON BEING ONE

Devotional Scriptures

> 1 Peter 1:13–25
> Titus 3:1–11
> Philemon 1–25
> Hebrews 13:1–25
> 2 Timothy 1:1–14
> 1 Thessalonians 1:2–10
> John 17

The Psalmist's Pen

> Psalm 133

FROM STEVE'S HEART

Do you ever wonder what it must be like to be the president of the United States of America? When I've had a long day at work or completed the execution of a difficult decision in the work place and feel worn out, I often think about the pressures of the presidency.

Of course there is plenty of information coming out of the Oval Office. The "talking heads," the White House Press Secretary, and speechwriters tell us what the president wants our country and the world to know. But what was he really thinking?

The Reagan Diaries by Ronald Reagan, edited by historian Douglas Brinkley, gives insight into the president's private thoughts and feelings and access to the unfiltered experiences and opinions of President Reagan in his own words. During his two terms as the fortieth president of the United States, Ronald Reagan kept a daily diary in which he recorded, by hand, his innermost thoughts and observations on the extraordinary, the historic, and the routine day-to-day occurrences of his presidency.

What if you had been alive during Jesus' life on earth and you learned of the plot to take him out? Imagine you came upon this quiet-spoken man—the one who had been stirring things up with His life and message—just before those who opposed Him, made their move. He's not clueless; He knew what was going on. What was on His heart? How would He pray? What would He say to His Father? His earthly life is about to end—if what He taught was true, there would never be another leader with such influence. What was He really thinking?

We learn far more than what a great world leader was thinking while in the Oval Office as we listen to Jesus' conversation with the Father that night; we hear His heart for us, His petition on our behalf that we be one. The Journey calls us to live together in *unity* for that is where God commands His blessing.

As you pursue life in Christ, ask our Father: *"What would You like to say to me today?"*

FROM THE FATHER'S HEART

Wholeness, oneness, unity of My People is a big deal to Me. Broken-ness, fragmented lives, rebellion, disconnected relationship ... that is not My design. From the start, all Creation was whole and good. Creation was characterized by unity and singleness of purpose, in accord with My plan. *One* ... complete and perfect, whole, intimate, connected, engaged, fulfilled ... that's My plan.

You can see what this would look like in our relationship by looking at My Son, Jesus. That's why Jesus told Philip, "To see Me is to see the Father ... the words that I speak to you are not mere words. I don't just make them up on my own. The Father who resides in Me crafts each into a divine act. Believe Me: I am in my Father and My Father is in Me." (John 14:6–11, The Message)

Oneness with Me was a big deal not only for Jesus but your Journey. That's what He was teaching when He used the vine and branch analogy. As you make yourself one with Jesus, the Vine so that His Word flows through you, you will ask for what you need and be heard. This is how I reveal to the world That I am … first through Jesus and now through you when you are one with Him.

I've spoken to you about loving others … the foundational command is to love one another. Oneness requires love … first you accept My love and then, love Me. You are to love others, too. This sets up the foundation for oneness.

Why is oneness so important? All who believe and choose to follow Jesus live in a hostile environment. What was created whole and perfect took a destructive fall through Adam's decision in the beginning and sin entered. The separation, brokenness, and disconnect is a result of man's rebellion. Jesus came to put all things, especially your relationship with Me, back together … followed by your relationships with others. Being connected, this oneness with other believers provides you protection from the hostility.

You live in a God-rejecting world which remains hostile to Jesus, the Truth, and the Message He delivered. So, all of His followers must be tight; one with Me through Jesus in order to live with My joy and purpose. Oneness with Us equips you to live well in a hostile, God-rejecting world without slipping back into rebellion yourself.

This pursuit of oneness is broad in scope and moves from your relationship with Us to your relationships with other believers. Jesus not only prayed for the original twelve but for all who would believe, for you. And what did He pray on that night before His betrayal: that you may be one.

Yes, I want you to become one heart and mind just as Jesus was one with Me and I with Him. And why is this so important? It's the plan. This influences the world that rejects Jesus. The oneness of all who believe makes it more likely that the world will believe, believe that I sent Jesus.

What was Jesus thinking about? What was on His heart about you that night? His focus in prayer was that all who believe might be one. He had experienced the hostility of the world and was about to feel the full impact of the cross. He also knew the power of oneness with Me. But He also knew your oneness with other believers would be a key to the world becoming whole … that you and other believers be one heart and mind with Us. As the world sees this miracle … one of the greatest miracles … it is so they will believe.

Do you understand why Jesus' prayer was focused on this theme? The impact of the Gospel on the world depends on all believers being brought into complete unity so the world can know that I sent Jesus and I love them.

Where does this oneness begin? It starts with your relationship with Me through Jesus so you have the ability to love others as I have loved you. Then, comes the unity and its agreement regarding one thing … Jesus, My Son, and your Savior. Seek My grace for your role.

I love you,
Abba

YOUR HEART

In your quiet time with God, ask Him this question: "Father, what would You like to say to me today?" Write what you believe He is saying to you. Write your name, and begin to capture whatever comes to mind, just as if God were speaking to you. For you see, He is …

Now, take a moment to write your thoughts to our Father.

Here are a few questions to help you as you reflect upon being one:

- What seems to stand in the way of unity today?

- How might you contribute to unity in your local fellowship?

- What role does the Body of Christ play in your spiritual growth?

- Why is the unity of God's people so important?

Prayer

Father, thank You for Your love for me as expressed through Jesus' death on the cross. Again I cry out for more of Your grace and to be filled with Your love. Help me to be one in heart and mind with You so my life and interaction with other believers makes it easier for the world to believe in Jesus. Forgive us, Your People, for the ways we fuss over stupid stuff, our agenda to the harm of the Gospel. In Your Son's Name, Amen.

Week 27

LIFE IN THE SPIRIT

Devotional Scriptures

Ephesians 4:17–32; 3:14–21; 5:1–18
Ezekiel 39:21–29
2 Corinthians 1:3–11; 8:1–15
1 Corinthians 13:1–13

The Psalmist's Pen

Psalm 104

FROM STEVE'S HEART

This past week I took a few days off to work on a significant landscape project in our backyard. Some twenty years ago I became interested in water gardens.

With my first effort I used common 10 mil black plastic for my liner and a green five-gallon green pickle bucket filled with lava rock to cover the sump pump for my "biological filter." The residents of that first little pond included: a small gar, a little catfish, and a perch, several water dogs and some goldfish, all compliments of Tommy Hicks Bait Shop. I was hooked.

My next pond had a real liner, used the same bucket and pump, but also had a commercial biological filter. Goldfish were the only invited guests to our backyard oasis. It was the next level and all before water features were hot on the scene of professional landscape designs.

Our move to Tulsa was the opportunity to create our third pond. Of course going to the next level was important. We built a ten-foot stream with waterfall and a nine-foot-by-twelve-foot pond. All the new pond technology was included with a professional pond kit designed to maintain a clear, beautiful pond…it was so fine people thought we hired professional landscapers to build it. Of course, going to the next level meant the addition of Kio fish. There were pond tours by this time. We returned to look over our pond, and much like God at the end of a creation day "we saw that it was good." Next level truly described the third backyard water feature creation!

You see, I have a great appreciation for nature—the combination of rocks, water, plants, and fish, the birds the water attracts, and the music the water makes as it finds its way over and around the rocks. Wonderful. Relaxing. Tranquil.

As you can tell, I started out pretty simple with this effort to imitate God in creation. Of course, that's where the idea came from; I saw what He created and wanted to imitate His work. From that first childlike effort to my latest "act of creation," there has been a maturity of imitation. What we began recently is our crowning effort: the plan includes a ten-foot stream with a five-foot waterfall cascading through a thirty-five-foot natural rock retaining wall. The rushing water will fall into a fourteen-foot-by-twenty-four-foot pond. This pond will be home to nine Japanese Kio (twelve to twenty inches in length) fish we raised from little fingerlings. Now that's next level.

Perhaps it is obvious, the analogy to The Journey…with childlike faith we come to know and accept Jesus Christ as our Savior and Lord. Life's seasons, temptations, experience of suffering or failure, and responsibilities increase our hunger for God; move us closer to imitating God. Life's fire refines us, and God's grace allows us to move to our next level of maturity—transformation into Christ likeness. We can only move in that direction by living in the Spirit.

Going to the next level? Just ask the Father: "*What would You like to say to me today?*"

FROM THE FATHER'S HEART

Life in My Spirit and love go together. If you want details on what love—My quality of love—looks like, go to the cross, and then read what I say in Scripture regarding the way of love. The only way you can love as I love is to live life in the Spirit.

The Journey is about putting off the old self and taking on an entirely new way of life—one I fashioned for you, renewed from the inside out, and working itself into your conduct, as I reproduce My character in you.

I created all the heavens and the earth, including you. My delight is to strengthen you by My Spirit living fully within you, giving you inner strength. Both of your feet are to be planted firmly on My love. As you live with others who believe, I want you to figure out and experience the extravagance of My love made know through Christ. You cannot discover the limits of My love—there are none. I want you to live fully in My fullness. I'm not here to take away but to give. Oh how I long for you to know Me as I am.

I can do this you know—create, fix, restore, forgive, give purpose and meaning, grant fulfillment and life, grant grace to live, receive and release love. I can do more than you could ever imagine or guess or request in your wildest dreams. Look at creation! Go to the zoo. Go deep sea diving and see. Go into outer space and see. Explore the cells of your body and see. Discover the mystery of the atom and see. Look at the hummingbird and the bald eagle and see. Yes, I am able to do immeasurably more than all you can ask or imagine, not by pushing you around with all My power, but by working within you through the Holy Spirit deep within.

This is really no great mystery. My ways are perfect. Creation, as originally intended, was marvelous…perfect. It's quite possible to be made new, to experience your very own "God-fashioned" life—to be made new in the attitude of your mind, Christ like.

The Journey is work. Transformation is painful, but moving from an empty-headed approach to living, ignoring the mindless crowd of voices to concentrate on hearing My Spirit, is worth it. To live the life you were created to enjoy is worth it.

So, how do you get there? By My Spirit and cooperating with Me. By completely giving yourself to Me. Watch Me and then imitate Me; you know how children learn proper behavior from their parents.

The Journey is about living a life of love—making progress through each season, each day learning to love as I love. I don't love in order to get something from you but to give everything of Myself to you.

Life in the Spirit means going to the next level—to maturity, the imitating of Jesus. As you do, all your family and human relationships will be impacted. How do you get to this level of living? By allowing Me to fill you with My Spirit.

I am committed to you, to your maturity as a human being and as a follower of Jesus. Can you live this life by trying harder? You know you can't. Life in the Spirit, My Holy Spirit, and the Spirit of Jesus is how you will live a life worthy of the calling you have received.

All you have to do is ask and I will make this faith-based experience a reality in your daily life.

I love you,
Abba

YOUR HEART

In your quiet time with God, ask Him this question: "Father, what would You like to say to me today?" Write what you believe He is saying to you. Write your name, and begin to capture whatever comes to mind, just as if God were speaking to you. For you see, He is …

Now, take a moment to write your thoughts to our Father.

Here are a few questions to help you as you reflect upon life in the Spirit:

- How might you connect what you see in creation to your life?

- When it comes to living as you were created to live, where would you like to see a change?

- Where has The Journey become hard for you?

- How might God, by His Spirit, help you move forward in obedience?

Prayer

Father, I want to thank You for the gift of Your Holy Spirit and how He comes along side to help me go to the next level as a follower of Jesus. I confess I'm sometimes content with just getting by and not cooperating with You as You come to take me to the next level. I trust You. I receive Your love and forgiveness and ask for Your grace to give You every part of my life every day of my life until The Journey is over. Here I am ... Teach me what it means to walk in the Spirit. In Your Son's name, amen.

Week 28

THE TRINITY

Devotional Scriptures

Deuteronomy 6:4–25
John 5:19–29
1 Corinthians 12:1–13
Ephesians 1:1–14
Colossians 1:1–14
John 16:1–31; 14:5–31; 15:18–27

The Psalmist's Pen

Psalm 80

FROM STEVE'S HEART

There have been a lot of different ways people have tried to provide analogies for God's self-revelation as Father, Son, and Holy Spirit. They all seem to fall apart as we try to use words with limited human experience tied to them to describe the divine nature.

John Wesley wrote: "You believe there is such a thing as light, whether flowing from the sun or any other luminous body. But you cannot comprehend either its nature or the manner wherein it flows. How does it move from Jupiter to the earth in eight minutes, two hundred thousand miles in a moment? How do the rays of the candle brought into a room instantly disperse into every corner? Here are three candles, yet there is but one light. Explain this, and I will explain the Three-One God." (As quoted in *A Guide to Prayer for all God's People*, pg. 194)

Theologians use the word "Trinity" to describe the nature of God. Trinity—the union of three: the Father, Son and Holy Spirit but one Godhead.

Recently I scheduled a team building lunch for the purpose of casting vision. A part of the conversation was guided self-revelation. I suggested everyone at the table had things going on outside the office that they bring to work; to be a team, the more we know one another the better our ability to relate with each other. For the most part they know me as boss, but they did not know my wife and I have three married daughters, five grandchildren (at that time), and that I grew up in Neodesha, Kansas.

God's self-revelation comes as Father, Son, and Holy Spirit. He wants us to know Him and has gone to great lengths to make Himself known to us.

Don't know where this is going in your journey, just ask the Father: "*What would You like to say to me today?*"

FROM THE FATHER'S HEART

How might I reveal Myself to you as one created in My image? The rest of creation just is; it is fulfilling its divine design purpose without challenge. I spoke and everything came into existence. Ah, but then came the moment when I created man—you in My own image. We decided to make you in our image, our likeness, to let the human race rule over all other creatures and to live off the land—and it was good, very good.

All the rest of creation accepted its place and My place. Then, with that creative act of making man "in our image" with intellect, free will, and self-government came the challenge. Not just for Adam and Eve but all who have come after, especially after they became enlightened by their act of disobedience.

So the question—how do I explain, reveal Myself to man, created in My image, rebellious and enlightened so you can know Me ... know My thoughts and ways, My love and purpose? I settled on the three-person-one-God revelation. I knew it would be pretty simple for you to understand: Father, Son, and Holy Spirit, especially once Jesus came, and showed you who I am.

It is a faith issue; some just struggle with such matters. Of course that's a little silly. If you believe in Me, then why not go with how I chose to reveal Myself to you? It's a faith proposition. I want you to know Me.

No one has ever seen Me, God the Father, but God the only Son; Jesus is the one-of-a-kind God expression. He has made Me known plain as day.

When it comes to My self-revelation and the manifestation of My presence in your world, it's a bit of a challenge to find the right words. All your words have experience-based meaning, which complicate your finite understanding. Although you were created in Our image you must also remember your thoughts and ways are not Mine. Just as the heavens are higher than the earth, so are My ways and thoughts higher than your ways and thoughts.

No one comes to Me, God the Father, except through Jesus, God the Son, and greatly added by God the Holy Spirit. Jesus came to you so you could know Me through experience ... historical, eye witness reports, and ultimately your own personal encounter. Even though no one has seen Me, to know Jesus is to know Me. Jesus revealed Me.

And just as Jesus revealed Me, the Holy Spirit reveals Him, thus Me. As the earthly life and ministry of Jesus came to a close, He promised that I would send My Holy Spirit. My Spirit continues to this day to make things plain to you and to remind you of all the stuff Jesus said and taught, revealing Me to you.

This all works together—love and knowing. First, you respond to My love, and then you can come to know Me through obedience to My Word. Jesus came as the Word made flesh to reveal Me and to demonstrate to you how much I love you. By faith you embrace

Jesus, accept and obey His teaching, and so demonstrate your love for Us. As you love and obey, you see. A loveless world is a sightless world.

Love Jesus, obey My Word that He communicated, and We will come into your life and make Our home with you. Don't love Jesus, don't obey My Word, and you're on your own—except, I'm going to continue My pursuit of you by My Spirit. I love you so much.

Indeed, I sent My Holy Spirit... to be your Helper, Friend, Counselor, and the Spirit of Truth to confirm everything about Jesus. As you know Him, you know Me. Keep it simple, and it is that simple. I have and will continue to make every effort to capture your heart and life with My love. And I am motivated to do this... look out for your best interest, because that's what love does.

My Spirit is active today. He is exposing the wrong thinking and beliefs of the world without Me. He reveals that 1) refusing to believe in Jesus is the basic sin; 2) righteousness comes from Me, from above where Jesus now resides out of man's sight and control; and 3) the prince of this world now stands condemned.

My Spirit will take you by the hand and guide you into all truth. His mission is to help you understand all this, not draw attention to Himself. Just as Jesus revealed Me to the world, He is to reveal Jesus. It's all about you coming to know Me, knowing My love, and living your life in response.

I am God—God the Father, God the Son, God the Holy Spirit; so revealing My thoughts and ways, Myself to you so you may have life, abundant and eternal.

I love you,
Abba

YOUR HEART

In your quiet time with God, ask Him this question: "Father, what would You like to say to me today?" Write what you believe He is saying to you. Write your name, and begin to capture whatever

comes to mind, just as if God were speaking to you. For you see, He is …

Now, take a moment to write your thoughts to our Father.

Here are a few questions to help you reflect on the Trinity:

- What is your response to the idea that God wants you to know Him?

- How do you view the Trinity?

- What thought stands out to you from today's reading?

Prayer

Father, thank You for Your revelation to us … to me. I believe in You, God our Father, Jesus, Your Son and our Savior, and Holy Spirit our Comforter and Counselor. I embrace who You are in my life. And still, I want to know You more. Grace me with a hunger and desire to know You as You are, not as I tend to make You out of my life experience. Help me. In Your Son's name, and by the power of Your Spirit, amen.

Week 29

TRUE FAMILY

Devotional Scriptures

Hosea 6:1–6; 11:11
Matthew 13:53–58; 21:12–17; 12:46–50
John 17:20–26
Galatians 1:11–24

The Psalmist's Pen

Psalm 40

FROM STEVE'S HEART

Four generations gathered around our Sunday dinner table—my mom and dad, me, two of our three daughters, and four of our five grandchildren. Yes, I know this was a moment and gift to be treasured. And yes, I know the family experience is different for every person reading these thoughts.

The influence of great grandparents, grandparents, and my parents allowed me to discover early in my life Who Jesus is and enter into a personal relationship with God. While not flawless, their journey gave me a faith-based worldview ... I am thankful.

Through my fifty-plus years of The Journey, God has been faithful, loving, and forgiving. Rita and I have been married over thirty years; our three daughters and their husbands are on The Journey. They are finding their way through the passages of life, as well. And as I previously wrote, Maggie, our first grandchild has in childlike faith accepted Jesus as her Savior; we wait in anticipation for the others. By God's grace, the faith-based impact of family continues through it all ... I am thankful.

Not only did our family gather on Father's Day, we participated in morning worship with our local church family. There is no question in my mind: my family is on the right track because of the influence of and our commitment to Christ's true family. Again, while not flawless, our journey with others of like faith has been instrumental in where we are along The Journey today ... I am thankful.

No matter what your experience with the family—earthly or spiritual—it is a part of The Journey. Join me in listening for what our Father has to say to us this week and ask: *"What would You like to say to me today?"*

FROM THE FATHER'S HEART

At its core the experience of family is about servanthood. Certainly there is the ancestry aspect, but it is really about relationships and how you interact with one another. When the servanthood principle of family is missing, that's when difficulties develop.

Servants serve others. By design, family members assist one another, promote the best interests of others, love one another, and serve. This is in line with My love and ways. My love is self-less; it is My commitment regardless of your response, and it is an act of My will, not feelings. This is true love. Servanthood is not only about loving one another, but about honor and obedience. Remember when Jesus was talking to one of those crowds? His mother and brothers showed up and wanted to get a message to Him. When told His family was outside He asked, "Who do you think My mother and brothers are?" Pointing toward His disciples He taught what it means to be family. "Obedience is thicker than blood," he said. "The person who obeys My heavenly Father's will is My brother and sister and mother—My true family."

You demonstrate you are true family members as you: serve others, love others, as Jesus taught you to love, and as you discover and do My will. Christ's true family embraces Jesus, the Messiah. Your faith in Jesus Christ places you in the family, not human ancestry or bloodline. "Obedience is thicker than blood."

And, remember when Jesus returned to His hometown? People gathered in the meeting place and He began teaching them just like He had in other places. The response was strange; at first they were amazed with His wisdom and miraculous powers. Then, they began to question and cut Him down because He was the carpenter's son; they had seen Him growing up as a neighborhood kid; they knew His mother and family; and they took offense at Him, "Who does He think He is?"

What's the point? Christ's true family members serve and love one another and believe. They did not honor Jesus in His hometown. What's the impact of this reaction? Hostile indifference limits what We can do in your life. The Journey requires more than lip service. It is your habitual trust in Jesus for your salvation and daily life that counts. The only thing that can limit Me is your unbelief. Jesus' ministry was minimized by His hometown friends and family, because they did not accept Him as My Son, the Messiah, and their Savior—thus, they rejected Me.

Bottom line, Christ's true family consists of people who accept as true His message, ministry, life, death, resurrection, and long-awaited return for His own. Welcome to the family! Your changed life becomes a song of praise to Me. Then many will see and fear and put their trust in Jesus and yes become members of Christ's true family. Your influence will be felt in the lives of others.

I am God the Father revealing My thoughts, ways, and expectations so you may have abundant life now and forever through Jesus Christ, My Son.

I love you,
Abba

YOUR HEART

In your quiet time with God, ask Him this question: "Father, what would You like to say to me today?" Write what you believe He is saying to you. Write your name, and begin to capture whatever comes to mind, just as if God were speaking to you. For you see, He is …

Now, take a moment to write your thoughts to our Father.

Here are a few questions to help you as you reflect upon being a part of Christ's family:

- How important is servanthood in your life experience?

- Where do you see servanthood expressed in your life?

- What is the power behind serving others?

Prayer

Father, thank You for the influences You have placed in my life Journey bringing me to this place along The Journey. Thank You for teaching me what it means to be in Christ's true family, by giving me the faith to believe in Jesus as my personal Savior. Grace me with the heart of a servant and one that loves others; grant me faith to believe what You say is possible. Thank You for my place in Your family, help me represent You well. In the name of Jesus, our Savior, amen.

Week 30
SIGNS OF THE KINGDOM

Devotional Scriptures

Matthew 3:1–10; 18:21–35; 20:1–16; 20:20–28
Luke 9:46–52
Acts 7:54–8:8
Galatians 2:15–21
1 Kings 19

The Psalmist's Pen

Psalm 84

FROM STEVE'S HEART

Recently I was given an assignment that has a potentially significant impact for the advancement of God's kingdom. About the same time this assignment came, I began to experience an unusual struggle. The best way I can describe it is to use the word *oppression*. Few knew of my struggle beyond my best friend and helpmate, Rita, but the spiritual opposition was great. Perhaps it was my commitment to write *The Journey* combined with the leadership role as Station Manager of a new Contemporary Christian Music radio station.

The previous week, one of my employees shared a conversation she had with several friends and listeners; each expressed how much they appreciated the radio station. They also spoke of their concern; that we were sure to encounter opposition as a result of the station's ministry.

She went on to relate the burden she had for all of us as she prayed for the station and in particular for me as the leader. Her thoughts were shared, not out of fear, but to raise our awareness. She was unaware of the oppression and what I now consider spiritual warfare.

In my journal Tuesday morning, I cried out to God...

"Abba, help me. You are my Shepherd, I trust You. Liberate me from this thorn bush and lead me beside still waters and green pastures. Open my eyes to see from Your perspective ... grant me discernment, to think clearly, show me Your ways ... Grace me to be a servant, a man after Your heart; purify my heart ... fill my heart and mind with Your Holy Spirit, Your love, Your life, Your thoughts and ways."

Wednesday evening, I shared the correspondence with Rita to get her thoughts. We discussed the challenges associated with the change of my responsibilities and my struggles with upper management. We could see the reality of what was going on and agreed in prayer for God to continue His protection and guidance for the glory of His Name.

The next day, I did not have a lunch appointment so I ran to Jamba Juice for a quick fruit-filled lunch. As I walked into my office, I became consciously aware that the "oppressive spirit" was lifted—I was set free.

In response to my need, God moved on the heart of another believer who obeyed His prompting and not only interceded in my behalf but related the story to me all the while not knowing what my response would be. God's kingdom is in the hearts and lives of people who are willing to submit to His authority over their lives. Thankfully, that is exactly where I am living today.

Will you join me in listening for what our Father has to say this week by asking: *What would You like to say to me today?*

FROM THE FATHER'S HEART

How long will you waver between two opinions? If I am God and Jesus is the Messiah, your Savior, follow Him. If the systems of the world rule and deliver ... let them guide your life.

Seek My face, My wisdom, and follow My leadership; bring Me into every part of your life. You do not have to be on your own—be bold and confident in Me; I am the Lord. I am God. Did I not create you? Have I not worked in the details of your life journey? Let your life be a sign of My Kingdom.

Do not fear man-made gods; they are mere imaginations and the temporal systems of this world—not God! People who worship hand-made gods call out, but no answer comes when it matters most. When the illusions are exposed, the reality is this: I am God, revealing Myself to you through Jesus Christ.

Do not be deceived and concern yourself with the world's pleasures—seek My face and be faithful to Me. Transformation is the goal. Peace is My gift. My joy is to be your strength. Servant hood is your pattern for human relationships. Self-denial is the path leading to the cross. Love is the greatest gift, love directed by your will with the best interest of others in mind. My kingdom is found where My sovereignty is embraced and not resisted—where Jesus rules in the hearts of people. It is not political. Let your life be a sign of My Kingdom.

Resistance is possible, but not eternal. I am God. The illusion is that man rules, that man is in control, that man is god. You know different so walk in it. Do not be discouraged, live your life under My authority and that will be a sign of My kingdom.

Joyfully embrace My authority as the Lordship of Jesus Christ manifests in your life as visible evidence of My kingdom. Your life, aligned with the Truth of My Word becomes ground for others to believe ... a sign of My Kingdom.

I am the Lord your God, your Light, and Protection. I bestow favor and honor. Look only unto Me; no good thing do I withhold from you as you walk in relationship with Me. You are blessed as one who trusts in Me, so walk trusting in Me today, and watch the impact.

Yes, the greatest sign of My kingdom is your changed life, the manifestation of the life of Jesus in your mortal body.

My kingdom was evident in Stephen's life. He was My messenger but the opposition arose and accused him falsely shutting their ears to My message. And yet, he reflected My glory as he spoke of Israel's history and My interaction with them. In the crowd that day there was one who stood by and watched as Philip was stoned to death. Indeed Saul was there, and he continued in his deceived state until he embraced My kingdom and with his changed life, later become the Apostle Paul.

Signs of the kingdom are not political. They are not tied to your success stories. They are not even the miracles. The *greatest sign* of My kingdom is when a rebellious and resistant person becomes a man or woman after My heart—the blind, made to see Jesus, the Way, the Truth, the Life, the hardened heart beating with love once again, the wounded and bitter living with the freedom of forgiveness received and granted to others. This is the greatest sign—your changed life. And when people see the transformation of your life, they have an opportunity to believe in My existence, accept My love, and embrace My eternal spiritual sovereignty.

I love you,
Abba

YOUR HEART

In your quiet time with God, ask Him this question: "Father, what would You like to say to me today?" Write what you believe He is saying to you. Write your name, and begin to capture whatever comes to mind, just as if God were speaking to you. For you see, He is …

Now, take a moment to write your thoughts to our Father.

Here are a few questions to help as you reflect upon observing God's kingdom:

- Where does the illusion of being in control show up in your journey?

- How real is the concept of God's kingdom in your thinking and everyday life?

- What would you like it be?

Prayer

Father, thank You for Your active involvement in our everyday, ordinary lives, that Your kingdom is not of this world, but that Your rule is not eliminated from this world ... we're not alone on our own. Today, I invite You to further establish Your sovereignty over my life, my home, my work, my pleasure, my hopes and dreams. Here am I. I embrace You as the King of my life. In the name of Jesus, our Savior, amen.

Week 31

GOD'S CALL AND PROVISION

Devotional Scriptures

> 1 Corinthians 2:1–15
> Matthew 9:35–10:15; 10:16–33; 10:34–42
> 1 Kings 19:9–18
> John 21:15–25
> Colossians 1:15–23

The Psalmist's Pen

> Psalm 8

FROM STEVE'S HEART

From time to time, the enemy seizes the moment to call into question the ministry expression of my life. I don't know if you can relate or not—it's actually a common comparison trap. The temptation is to assign a value proposition to different roles in life. Intellectually, I know and believe that every believer is a minister, but is my current assignment as important as a local pastor's role or a national religious leader, an author, or speaker? A narrowly defined ministry perspective leads to professional ministers' mentality and suggests everyone on this side of the pew has a lesser part to play.

Another expression of this potential for wrong thinking involves stories of salvation. Somehow it's more amazing when a murderer or drug addict accepts Jesus than when a child does.

God awakens and summons us to relationship, calls us to Himself, and then to serve Him with our entire life, heart, soul, mind, body, and strength by serving others. As the God who calls, He is also the God who makes available all things necessary to answer and fulfill our call. The Journey is an individual response to His call, followed by the acceptance of His provision to carry out His call with our lives. This is why we praise and worship God—He created us, calls us, and provides us with the means to know Him and live pleasing Him. Take heart: God does not make value judgments based on our role or assignment.

One part of the poem that became a great hymn of the church says it well:

> *Pardon for sin and a peace that endureth*
> *Thine own dear presence to cheer and to guide;*
> *Strength for today and bright hope for tomorrow,*
> *Blessings all mine, with ten thousand beside!*

> *Great is Thy faithfulness!*
> *Great is Thy faithfulness!*
> *Morning by morning new mercies I see.*
> *All I have needed Thy hand hath provided;*
> *Great is Thy faithfulness, Lord, unto me!*

Join me in asking the One who calls and provides: "*What would You like to say to me today?*"

FROM THE FATHER'S HEART

I ordained praise to silence the foe and avenger, to drown out enemy talk, and to silence atheist babble. Therefore, silence the enemy of your soul with praise. I am God.

Look at My creation, and stand in amazement of your position of favor in My plan. Do you realize I am mindful of you? I care for you. I have crowned you with glory and honor. All around the world, all creation joins in praise of My majesty. Don't allow those who fail to acknowledge Me deter your life of praise, worship, and obedience. Rejoice, My child, rejoice! Silence the enemy of your soul by lifting your praise to Me.

Take heart. Take hold. I desire to expand the influence of My purpose for your life and through your life. Rejoice My child that you can see what is yet to be in the advancement of My kingdom. I call you unto Myself from a place of alienation to the place of reconciliation through Christ's physical body and His death on the cross. Indeed, I summon all people to the pursuit of fellowship with Me and eternal life through My Son, Jesus Christ. Before you were even awakened to the call, I made ready The Way; reconciliation is available through Christ's physical body and death on the cross. By giving Himself completely at the cross, Christ has not only brought you over to My side but put your life together, whole and holy. I am the God who calls and provides—take heart! Would you walk away from such a gift? Or will you stay grounded and committed in total trust undistracted or diverted from My call? This is The Journey!

The message of the cross seems like foolishness to those who are perishing, those hell-bent on destruction. But when you accept My provision, it makes perfect sense. Providing is about being able to see forward and to prepare for what is needed. My Spirit dives into the depths of My ways, even the deep things and brings out to you what I planned all along. As you receive My Holy Spirit you can and will understand what I freely provide. With My Spirit you can accept the things that come from Me and understand them, since they are spiritually discerned.

People are harassed and helpless, sheep without a shepherd, just as much today as in the day of Jesus' earthly ministry. The need is great. The call is unchanged, and My provision is more than adequate. Ask Me, the Lord of the harvest to send out workers into My harvest field.

So where are you today? Level with Me, like Elijah did. Are you feeling tired, discouraged, like it doesn't matter...? Tell Me about it...

Allow Me to remind you: I call you, give you talent, and provide you what you need to be a difference maker in your world. I call. I provide. *See* where you are today is where I have placed you. Don't compare your assignment to that of another follower of Jesus. Live today with a commitment and belief that I have called you and your current assignment is a kingdom assignment. Look for an open door to take the foolishness out of the cross for someone who is perishing and deaf to My awakening and the Message.

I call you and provide you with what is necessary to be in right relationship—the forgiveness of your sins. I call you to ministry and furnish you with what is necessary to take the Gospel to the harassed and helpless. Call and provision. Called to love … to forgive … to be compassionate … to be holy … to live by faith … to rejoice … to wait … to trust … to be strong … to obey … to represent Jesus in your world. The magnitude of the call is exceeded by My provision—you have My Son, My Word, and My Spirit.

I love you,
Abba

YOUR HEART

In your quiet time with God, ask Him this question: "Father, what would You like to say to me today?" Write what you believe He is saying to you. Write your name, and begin to capture whatever comes to mind, just as if God were speaking to you. For you see, He is …

Now, take a moment to write your thoughts to our Father.

Here are a few questions to help you as you reflect upon the call and provision of God:

- What is the purpose of thanksgiving and praise in the life of a believer?

- How does praise and worship of God help you in a difficult time?

Prayer

Father, thank You for awakening me to Your call. First to hear and believe the Gospel and now to a daily life of ministry ... serving others and reaching out to those who have not accepted Jesus. Forgive me for my wrong thinking about what You value, and help me to tap into Your provision in order to be found faithful. Here I am Your servant. Grant me the grace to be obedient to Your call, and make a difference for Your name's sake. In the name of Jesus, our Savior, amen.

FOLLOWING JESUS HAS CONSEQUENCES

Devotional Scriptures

Matthew 12:46–50
Luke 14:25–33; 22:24–30; 9:57–62
Joshua 24:16–28
Romans 14:13–23
Galatians 5:1, 13–25
Proverbs 28:13

The Psalmist's Pen

Psalm 28

FROM STEVE'S HEART

Our backyard has a couple of eight-to-ten foot areas where the grass is dying—places where there is no grass. There are two-to-seven inch ruts, piles of stone, and rocks. It's a mess!

Along my journey, I noticed what happened when God took stones of various sizes, channeled moving water into a collection place, and added colorful plants, birds and fish, turtles and frogs. He flooded the entire scene with sunlight and shade. His creative handiwork really caught my eye and heart.

The messed up backyard I described is a consequence of pursing my dream to imitate God as we created a beautiful water garden landscape feature. We have invested long hours and some resources to pursue this dream. God has sent along help in our pursuit of this dream. It is a picture of The Journey.

I have seen Jesus revealed in Scripture, in nature, and through the lives of His followers enough that I want to follow Him with my life. The consequences of following Jesus Christ, in my experience, are all good, while not without cost.

Join me in asking the One who calls us by name: *"What would You like to say to me today?"*

FROM THE FATHER'S HEART

Let's begin with this: what does it mean to be a follower of Jesus Christ?

First you must decide for yourself who He is? Everything else naturally follows from your response to this core question. Is Jesus My Son, the Messiah? Was He born of the virgin Mary? Is He the Son of the Most High God?

Did Jesus lay down His life on the cross? Was He crucified, buried, and resurrected from the dead, just as He promised and eyewitnesses reported? The impact of what you believe about Jesus is the place of beginning. Pretty obvious, isn't it? You will not follow and align your life with someone you do not believe in.

Next you must decide whether the cost of following is worth it or not. What did Jesus teach? Simply put, you must be willing to take what is most important to you—everyone and everything—and give it? Nothing can be permitted to hinder your wholehearted devotion—people, plans, or even yourself. You must be willing to give it all up.

You do not have to do this unless you want the leadership of Jesus on The Journey. Be honest with yourself, for this decision has consequences either way. Evaluate for yourself. When you have followed your own guidance were you better off? Count the cost, but remember half-heartedness carries a cost too.

You believe in Jesus, My Son, your Savior, and the Messiah. You believe it is worth it to take up your cross and follow Him. Just one more thing: your faith in Jesus sets you free from being a slave of sin. Your surrender of everything, including yourself to Jesus, for He sets you on a lifelong course; you are made free to live the free life. Yes, with freedom comes responsibility; don't use your freedom as an excuse to do whatever you want, or you will destroy your freedom.

What does it mean to be a follower of Jesus? What are the consequences of taking The Journey? Your sins are forgiven, your life is surrendered to Christ, and you are free to be who I created you to be. As a follower of Jesus Christ, you are free to serve others in love. When you love your neighbor as yourself and love me with all your heart, soul, mind, body and strength, your freedom will grow too. What a marvelous consequence: the ability to live your life with other human beings under the leadership of My Spirit, free from the old sinful, self-directed, selfish self. Such a wonderful consequence!

I bring your walk of life in alignment with My ways. You live with a healthy affection for others, with exuberance for life, and true serenity. You develop a willingness to stick with things, have a sense of compassion in your heart and the conviction that a basic holiness permeates all of life. You find yourself involved in loyal commitments—not needing to force your way in life, exercising the ability to direct your energy wisely. Such is the consequence of following Jesus...living with love, joy, peace, patience, kindness, goodness, faithfulness, gentleness, and self-control. What an adventure, being transformed into the likeness of Jesus.

Of course there are consequences that come from trying to get your own way, too. Repetitive, cheap sex; a stinking accumulation of mental and emotional garbage; frenzied and joyless grabs for happiness; trinket gods; magic-show religion; paranoid loneliness; cutthroat competition; all-consuming-yet-never-satisfied wants; a brutal temper; an impotence to love or be loved; divided homes and divided lives; small-minded and lopsided pursuits; the vicious habit of depersonalizing everyone into a rival; uncontrolled and uncontrollable addictions; ugly parodies of community—such are some of the consequences of doing life on your own.

The consequences of following Jesus Christ are amazing once you see things from My perspective. Your Savior removes the sin that separates. You receive a way of life worthy of your total commitment, freed to love and respect yourself and others.

How do you see it?

I love you,
Abba

YOUR HEART

In your quiet time with God, ask Him this question: "Father, what would You like to say to me today?" Write what you believe He is saying to you. Write your name, and begin to capture whatever comes to mind, just as if God were speaking to you. For you see, He is…

Now, take a moment to write your thoughts to our Father.

Here are a few questions to help you reflect on the consequences of following Jesus:

- What does it mean to be a follower of Jesus?

- What is your first response to the concept of consequences?

- As a follower of Jesus, what area of your life has been most impacted?

- Where do you need God's help correcting the consequences of past decisions?

Prayer

Father, I confess Jesus as my Savior and rededicate myself to following Him. I embrace Your Holy Spirit's guidance and leadership and trust You to continue Your transforming work in my heart and life. Grace me to see life and my journey from Your perspective. Lead the way and I will follow. Here am I—take all of me, and grace me to walk in the freedom that is mine in the Lord, Jesus Christ. Grace me to be obedient to Your call and make a difference for Your name's sake. ... In the name of Jesus, our Savior, amen.

Week 33

MISSION & REWARD

Devotional Scriptures

Matthew 10:1–15
Romans 1:1–7
John 1:6–13
Colossians 1:9–23
Colossians 24–29
1 Peter 1:1–9
Galatians 6:7–18

The Psalmist's Pen

Psalm 35

FROM STEVE'S HEART

Rita and I returned from Neodesha, Kansas, and my class of '72, high school reunion; yes, that would be my thirty-fifth. About ten years ago, I began to embrace and value this trek back home as a part of my journey. As senior class president, it is my privilege to make comments, direct the dinner gathering on Saturday evening, and to entertain the faithful who show up.

In preparation, I pulled out my 1972 yearbook to refresh the memory and to get a little material for the entertainment. It's easy to be a stand-up comedian when you have such a willing crowd of people for material and as the participants.

You may find it interesting that most of those who showed up looked much older than I do. Seriously, how we think and how we live has a lot to do with how we age. The reward is sometimes observable, or so it seems to me.

My commitment to Christ was evident to all of my class mates back then, as it is today. It became sobering to recognize almost 20% of my high school friends from thirty-five years ago are no longer alive. So the evening included a moment of remembering, as Mike read the list of fourteen names of people gone from the seventy-two of us who graduated in 1972.

Then, I had forgotten what was printed on the inside back cover of our senior yearbook. Would you believe a passage from Ecclesiastes—the "time for everything" passage; I read it to them.

In simplest terms, I closed the reunion dinner by reminding them: "What you do matters. You have influence and can be a difference-maker. The past we can do nothing about, the future can only be influenced by our choices today."

The Journey reminds us of our mission and the reward which comes from being faithful to the One who created us and loves us. Join me in asking the One who calls us to His mission and promises us His reward: "*What would You like to say to me today?*"

FROM THE FATHER'S HEART

John the Baptist had a unique mission as the one chosen to announce the arrival of My Son, Jesus, the True Light. Your mission is the same, not in historical terms, but in redemptive history. There are still people who reject Jesus and ignore Me. So I need you to point them in My direction and to Jesus who is the Way, the Truth, and the Light … to help those searching for answers.

As one who believes in Jesus, you will be rewarded—made to be your true self, your child-of-God-self. All who receive and believe in My Son, Jesus, are given the right to become My children—not just born of natural descent, mere human decision or as a result of human intercourse, but born of My will. Rejoice.

Your mission as a believer is to deliver this simple message: the forgiveness of sins and reconciliation with Me is made possible through Jesus' death on the cross. It's all wrapped up in this one mystery that is now made known: all who have Christ can look forward to sharing in My glory.

You have a living hope, a brand new life, everything to live for including life after life, in My presence. Your reward is a life healed and whole, an inheritance that can never perish, spoil, or fade. With your focus on this, you can rejoice even when you're going through stuff, trials.

You believe even though you have not seen Jesus; you love and trust Him, rejoicing in My gift of total salvation. This is the reward of your faith. As one who has been made right with Me, you face life with joy moving ever closer to the long awaited day when we're face-to-face.

Here's what I want to do for you as a believer: I want you to enjoy spiritual wisdom and understanding, so you know My plan and will for your life journey. This allows you to live a life worthy of the calling and pleasing to Me; a meaningful, difference-making, purpose-driven life experience. I want you to know Me. I want you to know how I think and operate, so you can live well and be faithful in your assignment.

I want to give you My strength—not the grim, teeth-gritting, just hanging on response—but My strength that causes you to be amazed as you press through every obstacle and opposition to your obedience. My strength spills over into your expression of gratitude and joy once you recognized I am with you, through it all.

I want you to live today in this reality: you are rescued from the dominion of darkness and are a part of the kingdom of My Son, whom I love so much. Jesus brings you deliverance from the pit of sin and death. This is what I desire for you and such is your reward.

Allow Me to be clear on something, so you're not deceived: no one makes a fool of Me. Everyone will reap what they sow. Those who want a crop of weeds as their reward ignore Me and do their own thing. You desire a crop of life—real life, eternal life—so you are responsive to Me, seeking to please Me. It will be worth it, being faithful, so don't grow weary.

Boast only in the cross of My Son, Jesus Christ. The result of your identity with Him is freedom; freedom from the world and freedom from what men may say is the way. The single issue in all this is what I have done and what I am doing. And what is that? I am making you into a new creation.

Your mission, as one who believes in Jesus, is to pass along His message. You already know the satisfaction that comes from obedience. The Journey is leading you to your eternal reward. Don't grow weary.

I love you,
Abba

YOUR HEART

In your quiet time with God, ask Him this question: "Father, what would You like to say to me today?" Write what you believe He is saying to you. Write your name, and begin to capture whatever comes to mind, just as if God were speaking to you. For you see, He is …

Now, take a moment to write your thoughts to our Father.

Here are a few questions to help you reflect on your mission in life:

- How would you describe your mission?

- What adjustment(s) may be necessary to complete your mission?

- What role does a reward play in your daily decisions about an eternal reward?

Prayer

Father ... thank You for Your call on my life, for the gift of grace to receive the Gospel of Jesus Christ—the forgiveness of my sins through His death on the cross, and resurrection from the dead. Now, grace me this day to be faithful in my assignment as one who is sent to share this Good News with others. Open the door for conversation and moments of influence, by the power of Your Holy Spirit within me. In the name of Jesus, our Savior. Amen.

Week 34

GOD'S PLAN: TRANSFORMATION

Devotional Scriptures

Isaiah 55:1–13
Isaiah 1:10–17
Isaiah 1:21–26
Romans 15:1–13
Ephesians 4:1–16
John 17:20–26

The Psalmist's Pen

Psalm 46

FROM STEVE'S HEART

Plans, there are a lot of plans in life.

Before tearing out the twenty-five year old railroad-tie, retaining wall on Memorial Day, I could *see* the finished project. Remember, we had no landscape designer, but I have seen The Master's work, so the plan was in my heart.

The transformation of a normal backyard started with a consuming *heart desire* and *commitment* to imitate God's handiwork. Such desire led to *action*—a dedicated pursuit. All of this was spurred on the *hope* of a beautiful landscape feature, and the ultimate enjoyment we will have; is that what The Journey is about? Indeed, it serves as an illustration of God's plan for our lives.

As followers of Jesus and members of the body of Christ we must begin with the end in mind: to be like Jesus in our experience of life. The transformation begins with the heart desire to be in relationship; The Journey is supported by the people we surround ourselves with, the choices we make, and our ability to embrace God's grace to help us find our way.

Although I could "see" this incredible feature before I began, my knowledge of how it would come together was limited. For example, I did not know where the heavy duty equipment would come from or how it would be delivered to our backyard, or where the tons of stone and rock would come from, or how it would be delivered to our creation site, or where the muscle for some aspects of the job would come from or how weather—the rain and one-hundred-degree summer days would play a part, or how all the components would fit together. I hadn't done it like this before. But over and over again my Shepherd provided what was needed at just the right time. There is not near enough time to relate all the stories—but coming together, it is!

The word *plan* comes from a Latin word meaning "sole of the foot." God's plan is so much larger than mine. How about your plan? It is my heart's desire that the soles of our feet fall in line with His plan for our lives.

God has a plan for your life and mine. God has a plan for the church. He begins by showing us what it can be and asks us to get on board to accept His grace and His promise to help us find our way.

The Journey reminds us this week of God's plan and His invitation to be a part of something bigger than our lives and something larger than the local church. Join me in asking the One who calls us: "*What would You like to say to me today?*"

FROM THE FATHER'S HEART

Allow Me to remind you of this: I am your refuge and strength, an ever-present help in times of distress, affliction, danger, or need. So, there is no need to fear; don't be alarmed or agitated, no need for dread or apprehension on your part—no matter how it looks. I, the Lord Almighty, am with you. I am your fortress. Just observe the work of My hands.

Now, be still ... and know—recognize and understand this: I am God. Take time to recognize this reality, to know this truth and let it impact your thinking, your responses, your choices, your life, and your moment. I will be exalted above all things, people, or powers of the earth. Begin with this in mind.

So, what is My plan for the church?

Of course this is not about the local church—denominations, organized religion, as such—although this is applicable. The church is comprised of everyone who has been freed from the death penalty and punishment associated with sin—man's rebellion and thus, broken relationship with Me. It includes all who are forgiven and restored because of the sacrifice of My Son, Jesus—the Messiah who died on the altar of the cross, so you can be free. Yes, the church is made up of people who by grace have been saved, through faith in Jesus, not of their own doing, but as My gift. You are included in the church when renewed and re-created in Christ. Why? So you may join Him in His work. My plan is to include everyone. My plan is that through the church, My extraordinary wisdom will be made known to all.

Such strength of life is for service, not status. My plan is to develop maturity in you so you get along with others, especially one another in the church, just like Jesus would. I am the One who gives you living hope; let Me fill you with joy, fill you with My peace as a believer so the life-giving energy of My Spirit will spill over into hope.

The plan is for My people to get along with one another and the way to get there is to let Jesus be Master. The Journey from birth to death is to be lived under His Lordship. Let go of the judgmental, petty stuff that does not glorify Me—it's not My plan. My kingdom and the church are not about petty stuff; they're about how I work in your life, how I restore your relationship with Me, and then one another, making you whole and holy so you live with joy.

Your task is to serve Jesus with a single-mind. Use your energy to get along with others; encourage, don't find fault and drag others down. Share the life of Jesus, not your opinion on what the Christian life looks like. Develop your relationship with Me so your beliefs and behavior are aligned, and then I will use your life for My glory. You see, damage is done when you push your opinions and live with inconsistency while judging others.

Which brings Me to this: live your life worthy of the calling you have received that is to be a part of the church. The Journey is about running on the road I've called you to travel. Stay the course with humility and gentleness; make it a disciplined, steady pursuit. Pour yourself out for others with acts of love, being patient with others and alert to the differences, but not in order to make an issue of them. The church is called to keep the unity of My Spirit through the bond of peace. See to it that you contribute.

The church consists of those who have one hope and one Master, one faith, one baptism; those who embrace Me, the one true God and Father of all. Oneness is the plan, while the reality of individuality is present. You will not all look and speak and act the same—and that is a good thing.

My plan is that the church reaches unity in the faith and knowledge of My Son Jesus...to become fully mature, fully developed within and without, fully alive and free in Him. To help with this transformation, I have given prophets, evangelists, and pastor-teachers that they may help train all to be skilled servants while pursuing this unity I've spoken of.

Simply put, My plan for My people is this: that all who believe in Jesus, grow up and imitate Jesus, and demonstrate the transforming power of Jesus so that others come to know Him. Now, with this in mind go work it out.

I love you,
Abba

YOUR HEART

In your quiet time with God, ask Him this question: "Father, what would You like to say to me today?" Write what you believe He is saying to you. Write your name, and begin to capture whatever comes to mind, just as if God were speaking to you. For you see, He is…

Now, take a moment to write your thoughts to our Father.

Here are a few questions to help you reflect on God's plan for transformation:

- How do these ideas of God's plan for the church compare to your experience?

- What needs to happen in your life to see God's plan move forward?

- What needs to happen in your local church to see God's plan move forward?

Prayer

Father… thank You for the Body of Christ—the church and for Your plan, and for allowing me my place in it through my personal faith in Jesus. Have mercy upon us, and grant us grace to hear and to listen, to see Your plan, and then diligently seek You. Help me fulfill my place and contribute to Your plan for the church, even the unity Jesus prayed for, to the glory of Your name. In the name of Jesus, our Savior, amen.

Week 35

LISTENING

Devotional Scriptures

Mark 9:1–8
James 1:19–27
James 4:1–10
Romans 6:15–23
Philippians 2:12–18
John 14:15–24
Psalm 40:1–8

The Psalmist's Pen

Psalm 62

FROM STEVE'S HEART

It was late; I had just walked in from an outreach event at Driller's Stadium with Scott Dawson Ministries. "Safe at Home" is an outreach effort in cities with a minor league baseball team; a concert and evangelist service follows promptly after the ninth inning. They work closely with local churches to get a crowd out. Spirit 102.3 was their media partner; our morning show team was to introduce the music—Mandisa, of American Idol fame, and Building 429 were the guest musical artists for Tulsa, Oklahoma.

We had been out of town for the weekend. It was a ninety-five-degree Sunday afternoon and ... you get the picture. But I believed we were to get behind this as a radio station and that I was to be present. As the game went on there were a number of times I could have made an exit and done no harm; I just wasn't *free* to leave. So I stayed.

There was a positive response to the message. Dale, the KKCM promotion director, mentioned that there was a shortage of counselors—could I help out? So with the follow up materials in hand, I went to find someone waiting for a counselor. But then, Rebecca, co-host of the morning show, waved me over. She asked if I would work with the young man next in line. So I went.

Brandon had a drug addiction and was using pills to deaden his pain. He told me his folks were divorced, his finance's parents were divorced, and he did not have a job. He was hurting from life and reaching out for God. He acknowledged that he was trying to handle it with drugs instead of God; it wasn't working. He had been around the church enough to "know better," but just wasn't plugged in. So I prayed.

In an effort to prepare him for the inevitable attack once he left the stadium, we talked about being safe at home. I suggested that the next time the pain was too great to handle, he cry out to God and run for home plate, instead of away into left field, that he find someone he could call when tempted. Finally, I helped acknowledge that on Sunday, August 2, he cried out to God as he stood victorious at home plate.

We prayed for the same power God used to raise Jesus from the dead to be released into his life to win over the addiction of drugs. Then, it must have been the Holy Spirit, I said "Brandon, let's go stand on home plate." So we did oblivious of the people in the stands, and we concluded our prayer and conversation.

So, by God's grace, I listened and obeyed. And the reward was worth it … it always is.

The Journey reminds us of how important it is to listen and obey. To listen for His voice and response as we ask, *"What would You like to say to me today, Father?"*

FROM THE FATHER'S HEART

Find rest, be free from agitation, from being disturbed, and find My peace as you cease the constant movement and activity level of your daily life. Come find your quiet place in Me; your salvation comes from Me. Security and confidence, stability and protection are only found in Me. Will you make Me your rock, salvation, and fortress? Only then will you be unshaken. The enemy comes to oppose—it's part of The Journey.

Find rest in Me alone, and let your hope be fixed in Me. Let your confidence be in Me. The desires of your heart are fulfilled and will be expanded by Me in your life. When your reason for hope is securely placed in Me, you will not be shaken. Your salvation and your honor are tied to Me, your mighty rock, and refuge.

Obedience is impossible without listening. Obedience is the natural response of one who listens, desires to please Me, and receives My grace to live. Listen for the right voice—My voice.

Be still, so you can hear. Be still and listen for My voice, otherwise the busy attack will redirect your response to a reaction; your reactions are self, not Spirit-directed. Sacrifice and offerings are not what it's about, rather a pierced ear—an open ear prepared to listen and obey.

Wherever your path takes you today, remember this: be quick to listen, slow to speak, and slow to become angry. In your interactions with others, listen; try to hear Me, and don't be so quick to express yourself. Slow to speak, lest your selfish-self takes over with expressed feelings of anger, displeasure, hostility, indignation, or even exasperation. Such reactions do not bring about the righteous life I desire for you to have and enjoy. Accept My Word planted within you; listen much, so your obedience can increase.

Listening leads to action, otherwise you live in a deceived state of mind and life. Act on what I tell you, that's My expectation. Delight and affirmation come as a reward for your acts of obedience. Take My counsel, look into the free life I've promised, and pursue a life of obedience that is a blessed life.

Talking a good game is not My call on your life as My child. What am I looking for? That you reach out along your journey to those without a home or love and keep yourself from being corrupted by the godless world around you.

The pace of life…the distractions…the appeal and temptations of the temporal, the constant noise of so many voices—within and without—they all seek to disconnect you from Me. Each step of each day, I am engaged and eager to coach you and empower you to properly respond to whatever comes your way. But when we're disconnected, you become misguided; that's when you're wrong thinking produces reactions of the self-leading to poor choices. Guard your heart; your love for Me promotes your obedience.

Obedience leads to life or death, depending on the master. If you let sin tell you what to do you lose the so-called "freedom" to do whatever you please because you become a slave to sin. When you offer yourself to Me and allow My Word to guide you, your freedom never ends. The master you listen to determines the difference in your freedom. My instruction for skillful living will set you free to live large in My freedom. Sin promotes "do your own thing, don't worry yourself with God, and call your own shots—live free." It sounds good, but when you're honest with yourself, you know such a life leads to miserable slavery.

How different it is to live in the freedom I give—listen and obey Me, and your life is made whole and holy, ever expanding in new growth and newness of life; transformation into Christ likeness. If you choose to ignore Me and live a self-directed life, you won't bother with right thinking or right living as a slave to sin and self. But is that really freedom?

Good news! You do not have to listen to sin tell you what to do, which leads to death and separation from Me. You have tasted the delight of listening to Me in the context of our relationship. You know I love you and only desire what is truly best for you. Stay connected or life will push you around. Self will seek to rule your heart and the voices will seek to implant doubt during the tough times.

Listen to Me. When life is pushing hard on you, including common testing, challenges, and trials, consider it a gift. Why? Because you know that under pressure your faith in Me is forced into action ... out into the open.

So don't run, let the testing do its work in you, so you become mature and well developed, not deficient in anything. Sound good? Want that response? To respond well to the pressure of life's push-back requires connectedness. Here is what you do during your times of struggle and testing: talk to Me about it knowing that I love to help out. And My help is given without making you feel stupid or without putting you down for asking. Ask for My wisdom, and perspective, and grace, and strength, and help, and power, and joy, and peace—ask boldly, believe I am on it, and don't doubt.

How? Stay connected with Me by listening and obeying. You will be blown around during the testing times if you are filled with doubt. Be bold, determined, committed, and focused on trying to hear Me. Ask. Believe. Stay in position to listen and obey, and you will be amazed at the transformation. I will strengthen you with My joy as you pay attention and yield to My authority and act in line with My way of getting life done.

I love you,
Abba

YOUR HEART

In your quiet time with God, ask Him this question: "Father, what would You like to say to me today?" Write what you believe He is saying to you. Write your name, and begin to capture whatever comes to mind, just as if God were speaking to you. For you see, He is ...

Here are a few questions to help you reflect on listening:

- Are you a good listener? How do you know?

- If not, what makes it hard for you to listen?

- What is the role of questions in listening?

- Where in your life do you find yourself listening to other voices instead of God?

Now, take a moment to write your thoughts to our Father.

Prayer

Father, thank You for speaking so all can hear. Grace me to listen and obey. Help me not make our relationship so complicated, and help me not push You away or allow life to push You out of my daily life. Give me the desire to listen, to obey, and to be pleasing to You. In the name of Jesus, our Savior, amen.

Week 36

PROVIDED BY GOD

Devotional Scriptures

Genesis 22:1–14
1 Timothy 6:11–19
Psalm 68:1–10
John 10:1–18
Matthew 7:1–12
1 Peter 5: 1–11
Colossians 2:6–15

The Psalmist's Pen

Psalm 63

FROM STEVE'S HEART

You know I set out to build this pond as an imitator of God. I see His beautiful handiwork in nature; taking rocks and water and sunlight and moving water, and fish and birds to build a sanctuary. So the Kio pond in our backyard is a massive landscape project. But it is greater illustration of life, what true spirituality is—the imitation of God, resulting in transformation and new creations and beauty.

One additional life lesson out of this experience has been my complete confidence in God's ability to provide. The rest and peace that have been mine these past three months as we've labored over this landscape project have been amazing. Equally amazing has been

His provision of *how to* build it, some helping hands at just the right time, specific resources of equipment and ideas and tons of stone, physical strength, rain, and no rain—all at just the right time.

I say "at just the right time," because this has been one of those consecrated efforts. I firmly believe the vision was given to me, then the desire, and then the relationships; as everything was released into God's hands, He provided. He demonstrated over and over and over again, in this tangible project, how He has the ability to provide.

The Journey reminds us of how important it is to live our lives with total consecration and commitment to Him. This, so He can demonstrate His ability to provide whatever we need to be pleasing to Him. Listen for His answer as you ask our Father, "*What would You like to say to me today?*"

FROM THE FATHER'S HEART

Earnestly seek Me—demonstrate the truth of your declaration through a serious, purposeful pursuit. Do you ever get enough of Me? How deep is your hunger and thirst for Me? Even in the dry and weary land, do you hunger and thirst for Me?

In a time of worship, contemplate My power and My glory. Be still, and know I am God. Don't just give Me a head nod…deep crying to deep…I want you to experience intimate recognition and deep understanding within your inner most being. I am God.

Is My love better than life?

Will you earnestly pursue Me until your lips break forth and release praise to Me? Will you lift your arms like a banner, like a flag waving in whole-hearted surrender…waved in joyous celebration as one of My people…in praise of My activity in this grand event of your life?

In the dry and weary place, will you come before Me? See Me, and having recognized Me, will you find deep satisfaction and spontaneous praise with singing lips? When you are awake in the night, will you reflect on how I have been there for you and manifest a heart of gratitude? Have I helped you? Have I stood up for you? Then in this moment, be My child, free in My presence—take hold of Me, and I will hold you steady. Come, rest in My ability to provide.

The enemy of your soul will be dealt with ever so completely—that's My business. Come, rejoice in Me, and join with others who are committed to Me—lifting My praise! Why? This will silence the voices of the opposition, the voices speaking lies into your head. Say it out loud. Go ahead and make this your declaration: "Oh God, You are my God"… and now by faith, "earnestly I seek You." Go live in accordance with your declaration rejoicing in freedom and this rediscovered strength.

Like Abraham of old, I want you to keep moving, to walk in obedience believing I will provide. In salvation's history, I provided My Son, the "Lamb of God" to be sacrificed for your sins. When The Journey seems too much or the cost too great, keep moving toward the mountain of sacrifice, going without knowing at times, but confident in Me and My ability to provide.

Come, present yourself on the altar as an act of worship; give Me your all in recognition that I am God. Know, as Abraham knew, that no matter what the command or expectation, I will provide what is needed for your obedience. Have you ever asked Me for grace, but I failed to provide? Or did you just not ask, seek, or knock? Do you think I play games with you in your pursuit of living life? I love you.

When young in your faith you focused on the sacrifice required. Mature faith lets you focus on Me, knowing that whatever I require of you I will provide for your complete obedience driven by My love for you. And with your willingness to sacrifice, you are positioned to receive My blessing and an expanded vision for your life. My ability to provide is connected to your obedience.

Dare to believe I am able to transform any incident, any setback, any failure, and any disappointment into a grace-filled moment. It is what I do for those who seek My face. Own this and you will enjoy The Journey with a lighter load. I am God, actively involved. I see everything that comes your way and want to help you see it as an opportunity to respond to Me as I am present in that moment. As you embrace the reality that I am God of every moment, you will be positioned to receive the blessing hidden in those situations considered setbacks, unfortunate, unfair, and in fact, painful.

I want you to own your poverty. Awareness of your spiritual poverty will free you to receive more of Me, My wisdom, My life, and My ability to provide. Think about it, a person living in material poverty does not have to be convinced of their need. Neither do they have to be encouraged to be grateful when a need is met. When you are poor in spirit, no one has to teach you to cry out for help.

Poverty of spirit is an essential human experience along The Journey. Embrace your spiritual poverty to position yourself for a breakthrough. Acknowledge you're at the end of your resources, and the illusion of independence is exposed as you accept My authority. When light shines into your life and upon your relationships, you embrace My offer of a right relationship. Such fellowship is based upon you understanding that I am God, and you are not, and … you're good with that. What freedom comes with this simple childlike worldview—blessed are the poor in spirit, for you will see Me. My ability to provide will be made know to you along your life journey.

I love you,
Abba

YOUR HEART

In your quiet time with God, ask Him this question: "Father, what would You like to say to me today?" Write what you believe He is saying to you. Write your name, and begin to capture whatever comes to mind, just as if God were speaking to you. For you see, He is …

Now, take a moment to write your thoughts to our Father.

Here are a few questions to help you reflect on God's provision:

- How hungry and thirsty are you for more of God?

- What area of your life project requires you to exercise faith in God's ability to provide?

- What is "spiritual poverty" to you? How deep is your sense of "spiritual poverty"?

Prayer

Father, You are God, and I am not. I need You. Your call on my life is larger than my ability to imagine or execute. I ask You for a heart after You, a hunger and thirst for You, and a pure heart, so I may pursue a life pleasing to You—be glorified! Only Your kingdom is eternal. If not for Your grace, I cannot imagine the misery of my life. If not for Your grace, I cannot imagine the transformation yet to be! Thank You for the place of consecration and rest in knowing You are able to provide anything and everything I truly need to be pleasing to You. Praise Your holy name, amen.

Week 37

PRIORITIES

Devotional Scriptures

Luke 10:38–42
Romans 8:18–29
2 Corinthians 6:1–13
Revelation 19:1–8
Hebrews 10:19–39
Colossians 3:1–17

The Psalmist's Pen

Psalm 73

FROM STEVE'S HEART

How often have you heard or even found yourself saying something like this: "When it comes to life priorities, God is first, family, and then work for me"? The Journey is about saying and securing the most beneficial order of what I give my attention to everyday.

Have you started watching a movie where the title and theatre trailers or DVD cover promise a fine entertainment moment, but when it's over you think: "That was a waste of time?" Setting priorities can be like watching a "bad" movie … (okay, this probably has never happened to you) you keep watching, and you keep hoping the movie will deliver what the producers promised until you finally realize you just wasted ninety to 105 minutes!

Wasting time has to be one of life's major disappointments for me. Considering we don't know how much "time" we have, you would think we human beings would be all about making the best use of our time every day. But it is so easy to forget our days are numbered. And why is that? We're all so busy and so used to being so busy that we've come to accept that as normal.

The Journey is about God continuously drawing us unto Himself, giving us a hope that will not disappoint while teaching us to see life from His perspective. It is about receiving grace, so we make better choices today leading us to a brighter tomorrow. Ask God, our Father: "*What would You like to say to me today?*"

FROM THE FATHER'S HEART

Pay attention to what and who you're paying attention to—disillusionment is the result of looking in the wrong places for value and life definition.

Come into My presence to keep your life moving in the right direction. The winds of the world will blow you off course otherwise. Instant gratification is the enemy of maturity. Transformation is the objective of The Journey. Consistent choosing of My ways is critical to your progress; there are no shortcuts. Misguided thinking comes from an incomplete evaluation of the big picture. Never forget there is a conflict between the temporal and the eternal; confuse them and you will be confused.

Come in your weary-with-the-success-of-the-world observations. When tempted with envy at how their lives appear to be filled with ease, let Me take your hand; I will lead you back to the path and bless you with more of Me. Come into My presence, and let Me help you clear your head. Allow Me to help you see what you cannot see from a limited perspective.

When thinking clearly, what do you really want in life—if not more of Me? The Journey will wear you out, but not "down and out" as you make Me the strength of your heart; come pursue knowing

Me. The reality is this: destruction is waiting on the unfaithful. As for you, My child, it is good to draw near to Me, especially in times of misguided thinking. I am the Sovereign Lord. Let Me be your refuge.

You are invited to sit in My presence listening, soaking, waiting, and resting... this is our time. There are more than enough things and voices that will try to turn you from your focus upon our relationship and your spiritual development. Be on guard for that which seeks to pull you away, not just from our regular quiet time, but also from Me. Distractions abound, and it comes down to a value question. I'm not rigid about this, and you must decide if all the "preparations" have to be made or not.

Recognize this—the more you allow distractions to pull you away from Me, the more unstable you become. This leads to unstable thinking and a false image of who I am. When you're fussy and worried and worked up over nothing (nothing in the big picture of eternity) you're disconnected.

Life is full of choices, more stuff to do than time to do it all. That's why I give you this guiding principle: only a few things are necessary, and really only one. Mary chose the essential and it could not be taken away from her—to enjoy an encounter with Jesus.

Note the empowerment and strength that come to you when our face-to-face time is a priority.

What is required to establish right priorities? First you must have hope; you must know what's coming next; your full deliverance and complete salvation is near. Your present hard times are truly nothing compared to the coming good times, trust Me.

Hope let's you wait in joyful anticipation. My joy gives you strength as you wait. But when you grow tired in the waiting, My Holy Spirit is right alongside you to help you stay the course. Then you can choose what is in alignment with My ways; make your steps firm while you keep first things first.

I know you, your journey, the pain, and the potential weariness; I know you better than you know yourself. So My Spirit helps you in your weakness to keep aligning and realigning your heart, your thinking, your choices, and your steps with My will.

Have confidence in My ability to take every detail and work them into something that benefits you, even when you can't see it right away. Keep your hope alive about the future and being in My presence; this will help you establish kingdom priorities.

The other thing to keep in mind is My vision or purpose for your life. From the outset, My intent has been to transform your life. You were created to be like Jesus. Setting right priorities is easier when you remember the main objective: I will shape your life, as one who loves Me, along the same lines as Jesus' life. And know this; I am sticking with you to the glorious completion of what I've begun. Will you cooperate with Me in this? This is what establishing right priorities are about—helping you along The Journey until you are home with Me. How do you know I'm committed to you in this? I did not spare My Son's life, but gave Him up for you; I'm in. Never, never doubt My love and commitment to you no matter what; I'm on your side.

Keep your living hope alive and My purpose for your life in mind and your ability to prioritize life will be greatly enhanced. Make life choices—how you use your time, your gifts, your resources, your skills, your presence in light of eternity knowing My intentions to shape your life along the lines of Jesus' life.

Your priorities shape your responsiveness to Me, My call on your life, and the quality of The Journey. Right priorities follow right priorities. It's a lot like walking—each step moves you closer to the destination.

I love you,
Abba

YOUR HEART

In your quiet time with God, ask Him this question: "Father, what would You like to say to me today?" Write what you believe He is saying to you. Write your name, and begin to capture whatever comes to mind, just as if God were speaking to you. For you see, He is...

Now, take a moment to write your thoughts to our Father.

Here are a few questions to help you reflect on your priorities:

- How well do your priorities guide your decisions each day?

- What adjustment(s) may be necessary to start living by priorities?

- How does your hope of eternal life impact your priorities in life?

Prayer

Father, I thank You for continuing to draw me to yourself. Forgive me for the poor use of my time and misguided priorities. Grant me grace to live by right priorities today and to make the best choices possible, for it is my desire to be pleasing to You and to glorify You. Praise Your holy name, amen.

Week 38

LIFE'S UNCERTAINTIES

Devotional Scriptures

Isaiah 54:9–17
Hebrews 10:1–10
2 Peter 1:1–11
1 Peter 3:13–22
1 Peter 4:12–19
John 17:1–19
Hebrews 11:1–19

The Psalmist's Pen

Psalm 127

FROM STEVE'S HEART

Today, I ask God how I could introduce The Journey this week.

He directed me to spend time reflecting on my history. So I went to the inside cover page of my Bible, where I record the more significant historical dates of my journey. Twelve years ago, this month, a major change of direction came my way, which resulted in moving my family to a new city and eight, long months of waiting on God—without a job. Talk about a "no man's land" experience; I was in the darkest night of my journey.

Now twelve years later, what do I see? Here's what I wrote in my Journal to God:

"Wow, a lot of life and yet, a simple life; not simple compared to my parents and grandparents life-style, but in the grand potential of life relatively straight forward. Moving towards fifty-three years of life I'm married to Rita, my best friend (thirty-one years, next month)

… our three daughters have faith-based relationships with You and married men they love

… we have five precious grandchildren

… we have good health

… there is purpose and opportunity in my work; You have blessed me and made it work out, through it all! Here am I, steadied by Your hand as I stumble forward—praise Your Holy Name.

The Journey calls us to move forward through each season of life confident in God and maintaining hope regarding eternity while boldly facing the temporal uncertainties of life on this planet. Will you ask God, our Father: *"What would You like to say to me today?"*

FROM THE FATHER'S HEART

To manage life you must be connected, in touch, with Me. To be connected requires consistent time together, and you to be clear minded, self-controlled. This will allow you to enjoy an effective prayer life and to handle the times you live in.

There are three causes of uncertainty, trouble, or difficulty on The Journey:

1. that which is just life lived in a fallen world

2. that which is self-inflicted, and

3. that which is a result of your commitment to Me in a world resistant to My kingdom.

No matter the cause, don't be surprised with the trial or difficulty and jump to the conclusion that somehow I'm disengaged. Keep in mind Jesus' journey. Remember My purpose is about your transformation from selfish, self-rule, self-government to Christ likeness and submission to My will and authority. This is a spiritual refining process with glory just around the corner.

Jesus went through everything you could ever go through and *more!* Learn to think like Him. Learn to see suffering as My way of moving you from the old sinful habit of always expecting to get your own way. My goal is your freedom. I want you free to pursue what I want for you instead of being jerked around by what an out-of-control-self wants in this upside-down, rebellious world—nothing but a dead-end street. However, if things are difficult because of your obedience to Me, take it in stride. Keep placing your trust in Me; I am faithful.

Look at Jesus and the example He is in this. The time had come, His betrayal was near; falsely accused, rejected, abandoned, the most severe beating a human being could imagine, and then crucifixion. How did He talk to the disciples as He faced all this?

He laid out the truth; difficulties are a part of The Journey. He invited them to totally trust in Him, so they would be unshakable and assured, at peace. He assured them with the foundation of their confidence and hope in facing life's uncertainties—"Take heart! I have overcome the world."

So it remains to this very day in your life. In this world you will have trouble. Receive My peace, so you can remain unshakable as you place your trust in Me. And take heart, Jesus conquered death to set you free.

Notice how Jesus faced the darkest hour any human could imagine; what does it look like? He remained connected to Me; He had no question as to whether I was with Him or not. He remained clear-minded and self-controlled, so He could pray.

Winning the battle for your mind is critical to your ability to face life's uncertainties. It doesn't matter if the difficulty is persecution due to your commitment to Me, or consequences due to your choices. Self-inflicted, or the tribulation which comes with living on the earth—you must remain connected to Me to be victorious.

Misguided thinking, subjectivity, the lies and taunting of Satan and all those voices are designed to steal your joy, peace, and bravery, your hope and confidence in Me. When your heart is committed to Me, Satan will attack your mind using life's troubles and uncertainties to sow seeds of doubt and fear. Stay grounded and close to Me, and we'll get through it.

Now, listen to Jesus pray. How did He face His darkest hour victoriously? He focused on My purpose for His life and truth. Eternal life is knowing Me, the only true God and Jesus, My Son. Then, He focused His attention on the need of others. Profoundly simple, but effective and you can have this same response by My grace—just ask.

There's nothing quite like a historical review to bring perspective and assurance to the moment. Fundamental to facing life's uncertainties is your ability to place your total trust in Me. Such a response is fundamental to your journey as you walk, run, rejoice, sit, wait, rest, weep, celebrate along the way. Once you are sure of what you hope for to the point of being certain of what you do not see, you're at a place where you can stand—even in the face of what appears uncertain. Such faith gives you a handle on life, especially as you face stuff that threatens your peace, your hope, and your confidence. The Journey is meant to be lived out on this firm path making life doable.

Faith gives you the ability to see Me behind Creation, including you and your life. The ability to respond to life in faith is what distinguishes you from the crowd in the same way other men and women of faith have done.

By faith, Abraham said yes to My call on His life. He, too, made The Journey going without knowing where, just the Who—totally trusting Me. So it is for you.

I love you,
Abba

YOUR HEART

In your quiet time with God, ask Him this question: "Father, what would You like to say to me today?" Write what you believe He is saying to you. Write your name, and begin to capture whatever comes to mind, just as if God were speaking to you. For you see, He is …

Now, take a moment to write your thoughts to our Father.

Here are a few questions to help you reflect on life's uncertainties:

- How have you been surprised by a trial or difficulty in life?

- What promise from God are you leaning on in order to persevere?

- How do you tap into the "joy of the Lord" for strength?

Prayer

Father, I thank You for giving me a place of rest as I trust in You—no matter what! Thank You for Your mercy and forgiveness when I bring difficulty on myself by poor choices, for protection and provision for The Journey which just includes life in a fallen world, and for grace when my allegiance to You brings pressure from people and systems of the world. I receive Your joy and peace as I place my total trust in You during my life's uncertainties. Thank You for Your help along The Journey. In Jesus' name I pray, Amen

THE MYSTERY OF GOD'S GIFTS

Devotional Scriptures

Matthew 8:1–4; 8:5–13; 8:14–17; 9:18–26; 9:27–34
Mark 10:46–52
Hebrews 12:1–2, 12–17
Jeremiah 19, 20

The Psalmist's Pen

Psalm 145

FROM STEVE'S HEART

This is my real world … it is what it is … I can do no other; last Tuesday's Journal entry follows:

Abba, You are my Shepherd—I will not live in fear regarding the future or what man can do to me; You are my Sovereign Lord. Hallelujah! My steps are ordered by You—I will not be anxious about my calendar.

Jesus, You are my Savior—I will not be a slave to sin.

You are God Almighty, the beginning and the end; faithful, just, and righteous—I will embrace Your joy, Your peace, the righteousness of Jesus and totally trust You … Hallelujah!

That was a week ago on the Tuesday *before* a close of business meeting on Friday; I was informed that due to budget cuts, my position was being eliminated for 2008. I had just lived my last day as Station Manager (I just didn't know it). I would now pack my office. I would need to call Rita for a ride home (I had a company car).

Shock and awe!

The mystery of God's gift...

This past Tuesday, we sent Monica, our middle daughter, and grandson, Kalen, to Mexico, so they could re-connect with Severiano—husband and dad. You see, several years ago, Severiano was *legally* working and living here in America; they met, grew to love each other, and married. They now continue to wait for a waiver, which they were told would take three-to-six months. It's been sixteen months of separation. Money they didn't have has been spent on immigration specialists and attorneys only to be given inaccurate and incomplete counsel. The political football of immigration is more than just another news story for our family. Day after day, week after week...we wait.

The mystery of God's gift....

We returned home from Oklahoma City to receive word from our oldest daughter, Stephanie that she was heading to the hospital to deliver her fourth-born child and our sixth grandchild. Max Steven made it, but had some breathing/lung challenges. He was transferred to the Baptist Hospital NICU. But, in mercy and grace, he is a candidate to be dismissed tomorrow. Yes, we're grateful—and yes, we understand there are families by the thousands with routine deliveries and thousands waiting for a good report on their little one.

The mystery of God's gift....

Life can simultaneously arouse and elude our desire and ability to comprehend or explain—it's the mysterious stuff of our lives. Your story is no exception, most likely.

No, I still don't know what's next for me vocationally, but I was able to spend the past week in Oklahoma City helping Stephanie and Jeffrey and our grandchildren in a time of need. There have been numerous phone calls and personal notes from a substantial group of people—a means of grace in our lives during this mysterious change in my career-work-ministry-life.

My life has been expanded this past week through the events I've briefly described. My heart is:

…more tender to those with health related situations and appreciative of the professionals that seek to bring healing to the afflicted of our planet;

…more sensitive to our children going to school and appreciative of the professionals who feel called to teach and help educate our children;

…more aware of the demands on families today, the pain of those lost in the crowd and broken systems of government;

…encouraged by the power of an encouraging word—even when someone did not know what to say, but they reached out to me anyway;

…more committed than ever to be a man after God's heart and to find His purpose for my next chapter knowing all I want to do is help people know Him and receive His grace for this mysterious thing we call life.

By God's grace, I'm filled with hope and forgiveness in what has been one of my top two toughest moments along The Journey. The *greatest* mystery involves God's love for us; how He gave His one and only Son so that whoever will believe in Him shall be saved.

The mystery of God's gifts….

Yes, I know you have your story too. In fact, it may make mine look like child's play. No doubt someone is reading this and wishes for such an "easy week" as I've just experienced. My heart truly goes out to you. What is common ground for all of us is how The Journey calls us to move forward through each season of life confident in God and maintaining hope regardless of the mystery; life on this earth may present us God's gifts.

Will you ask God, our Father: "*What would You like to say to me today?*"

FROM THE FATHER'S HEART

The most difficult thing to understand is how anyone could see My Son Jesus, rejected, crucified, ridiculed, and put to death on a cross and still rejects Him as My gift, the Messiah, your Savior. You cannot imagine My position, what it is like to be Me—all knowing, all powerful, everywhere present, great beyond greatness—but rejected. Still I remain gracious and compassionate, slow to anger and rich in love toward you—compassionate to all I have made, waiting, yes, waiting, to receive your love in return. Is that a mystery to you? It is true: I love you.

I'm sorry for the difficulties of your life, but I remain your Shepherd. This is a small thing for Me. I want you to raise "a stone of help"…you are Ebenezer and like Samuel of old declare, "*Thus far has the Lord helped us.*"

As you seek to imitate Me, you find it takes hard work, but I really want you to allow Me to be the Provider and Overseer of the process. We will work on what is next, so you can begin to see it with the eyes of faith. Then we will enter into action, the hard work of creating what is yet to be. I will be project manager releasing resources at just the right time. Hold on to the stories of My faithfulness in the past, as we move forward through the opposition of your obedience and acts of faith towards your future.

The mystery of My gifts—yes, there will be events in your life that are not fully understood or understandable from your view point. Remember My commitment to give you revelation, so you can begin to comprehend greater truth, not necessarily the *why*. This is the other aspect of mystery—spiritual truth comprehended by divine revelation.

When faced with a mystery that does not seem to be a gift, remember the mystery of My love and forgiveness, and be thankful. Then, you will see the gift.

I love you,
Abba

YOUR HEART

In your quiet time with God, ask Him this question: "Father, what would You like to say to me today?" Write what you believe He is saying to you. Write your name, and begin to capture whatever comes to mind, just as if God were speaking to you. For you see, He is…

Now, take a moment to write your thoughts to our Father.

Here are a few questions to help you reflect the mystery of God's gifts:

- Can you recall a *surprise?* How did you respond?

- If it is in the past, how did things turn out?

- If you're still in it, what does your faith invite you to do?

Prayer

Father, I confess my tendency to evaluate most stuff in light of how it impacts me. Purify my heart and teach me to be less self-centered. Grant me the grace to be more in alignment with Your kingdom, Your will, and Your purpose. Help me be a means of grace to another human being, who in their hurting state, stubbles across my path. More of You, less of me; even a cup of cool water given in Jesus' name… In the name of Jesus, our Savior, amen

Week 40
THE CENTRALITY OF CHRIST

Devotional Scriptures

John 1:19–28; 14:1–11
Colossians 1:15–23
John 6:66–71; 12:20–36; 11:1–16
Luke 13:22–30

The Psalmist's Pen

Psalm 18

FROM STEVE'S HEART

A couple of weeks ago, we introduced three of our Kio to the pond. At first they were very responsive. One night, after their arrival, I set up a work light so we could work late into the evening. The next day(s) they remained aloof, running from me instead of to me when I came to the pond to feed them; they went to the bottom of the pond to get away from me. You may be able to imagine the disappointment.

Two weeks later we added three more of our Kio to the pond. One of them, Goldilocks, is by nature friendlier and has a soothing influence on the others. (Seriously, that is what the man at Kio Country told us about the breed.) So there are six fish in the 3,500-gallon aquarium in the ground. Sure enough, now all of them swim to greet us when we walk out to the pond and feeding time is such a delight, once again.

Keep in mind these are two-four pound fish that have been "boarded" at Hardscape Materials the past fifteen months until we could build their new home. I have really been looking forward to having them around to enjoy once again. They were fingerlings when we bought them. We have worked *hard* the past three months to build this pond for them to enjoy.

Yesterday, Goldilocks, Phantom, Niki, Dolphin, Old Yellow, and Sherbet were very responsive at feeding. It was a fun, rewarding, and fulfilling moment; that's when I had a God-moment.

"This must be a little something like it is for our Father," I told Rita. "We've spent months working hard to build this pond for our fish. We want them to enjoy it, and all we want is the opportunity to enjoy them, too. How disappointing it was when they rejected our presence. I'm so glad Goldilocks has led the way for the group to change their behavior." I went on, "It's like God, He created this great place for us to live and only wants us to enjoy it and fellowship with Him—how hard it must be when we reject His efforts."

Scripture is clear that our ability to enjoy life and find meaning and purpose in life requires a personal relationship with Jesus Christ. There are many things and people and pursuits that seek to take the place reserved for God in our lives. The Journey calls us to keep Jesus at the center of our lives, our relationships, our plans, our hopes, and dreams for this life and our life after death.

What or who occupies center stage in your understanding of life—your heart and life? How do you manage your best times or those tough times? Who rules your heart, and mind, and soul, and body? What will you say at the end of your earthly existence when God, the Father, inquires about why you should be allowed into His presence for eternity? The centrality of Christ is the New Testament message about how to enter into a relationship with God and The Journey. Will you ask God, our Father: "*What would You like to say to me today?*"

FROM THE FATHER'S HEART

I hope you are enjoying the beautiful fall days. Please receive the rain, the beauty, and refreshing cooler temperatures as My gift. Enjoy!

I am your strength. Yes, I use networks of people, talent, gifts, and experiences—but remember: I am your *strength*. In My strength, you can have power to withstand strain and stress. You will have power to resist attack; in Me, you are strong.

Let Me be your rock, your fortress, and your deliverer—come, take refuge in Me. Call to Me that I may save you from your enemies … fear, misguided thinking, anxiety … all the stuff that will try to deliver a destructive impact on your life and relationships.

Let Me assure you, I have heard your distress cry; I have heard your voice during this, another moment along The Journey. Watch your focus, so you avoid feeling overwhelmed, like you're going down. You are not.

I am not pleased with all the details of this situation that I've permitted. If you could see clearly, you would be amazed at My response. You will see for I have reached down to take hold of you—just like in the past, I will again, drawing you out of deep waters. I will rescue you from forces too strong for you to handle. They have taunted you in the day of your disaster, but I was and I am your support.

Know this: I have brought you out into a spacious place with each disaster. This time will be no different. You will see how vast in scope the new place will be; it will offer you more space and room—yes, a spacious place.

I rescued you, because I find great pleasure and enjoyment in you. It is true; I love you. I am pleased to be in your life; I am in your corner. I am God.

In this age, since Jesus' birth, crucifixion, and resurrection, I treat you according to the righteousness of Christ. Even in your pilgrimage of transformation the critical factor is this: you have not done evil by turning from Me. My reward is given to you based upon how I see you, not other's views. Remember this as well as you look upon others. It is the righteousness of Christ that presents you to Me, acceptable in My sight.

This journey is also impacted by how you see Me. I am God, so how you think of Me only changes you, *not* who I am. So remember...

...to the faithful, I am seen as faithful,

...to the blameless, I am seen as blameless,

...to the pure, I am seen as pure; but

...to the crooked, I am seen as shrewd.

Humble yourself before Me. It is the proud who are brought low; those who do not want to know Me, cannot figure Me out. I turn your darkness into light; let Me keep your path lit, so you can be victorious in battle.

Never forget My way is perfect, straight, and smooth, even when it does not feel like it, it is;

...My Word and direction are flawless, proven; just keep running toward Me and take refuge in Me, you will make it;

...there is no other God beside Me; you've found rock-solid footing in Jesus Christ, your Savior;

...I have armed you with strength and make your feet move forward in the right direction. Indeed, as one who pursues knowing Me, and as one totally surrendered to Me, I am making your feet like those of a deer—sure-footed, perfectly aligned for climbing to new heights;

...I have trained you for this battle; seek My face, be still before Me, listen, and record My insights to you and victory is yours. Prayer is your most powerful weapon; listen much, and speak also;

...in Christ, I have given you salvation-armor and My right hand holds you up, sustaining you; I have great compassion for you and take delight in you. Listen, I've cleared the path so you need not fall.

You are victorious, for I am your God; granting you victory, deliverance, and favor. I will set things right for you. Will you worship and rejoice in Me?

You are in right relationship with Me, because of your faith in Christ alone. He is the Way, the Truth, and the Life. No one comes to Me, but through Him. The Journey demonstrates His ministry of reconciliation on your behalf.

I love you,
Abba

YOUR HEART

In your quiet time with God, ask Him this question: "Father, what would You like to say to me today?" Write what you believe He is saying to you. Write your name, and begin to capture whatever comes to mind, just as if God were speaking to you. For you see, He is ...

Now, take a moment to write your thoughts to our Father.

Here are a few questions to help you reflect on the centrality of Christ:

- How are you tapping into God's strength along your journey?

- What does your spacious place look like?

- Where are you living today—in your spacious place or a difficult place?

- What needs to happen to move forward?

Prayer

Father, I confess there are many things or people that seek to take center stage in my world. Forgive me. Once again, in faith, I confess Jesus Christ as my Savior and Lord of my life. Take Your rightful place of power, influence, and control of me, my heart, soul, mind, and body. In the name of Jesus, our Savior, amen

Week 41
TRUE DISCIPLESHIP

Devotional Scriptures

Philippians 2:1–8
Galatians 5:16–24
Matthew 5:1–16; 7:21–28; 5:43–48
John 1:1–18

The Psalmist's Pen

Psalm 1

FROM STEVE'S HEART

Seems like Rita and I are candidates, or should be, for our own HGTV show! How many times have we restored a place to make it our home? How many landscape features have we built? Maybe not enough for our own series, but a few good shows! How about, "Devise on a Dime with a Design"?

We were recently at it again—not the "Extreme Makeover" game, but intense enough. Rita's mom loves her daughter's hand texture, so off to Kansas we went with creation tools and mud in hand. She just wanted a couple of rooms textured and that included painting, of course.

There was no added pressure as we helped select paint color at Woods Lumber Company. The tile and floor covering had already been selected. Can you imagine Betty (a woman of strong opinion),

Rita (the ultimate peace maker, meek and mild), and Betty's self-declared "favorite son-in-law" (that's me) evaluating the best color schemes, while John (E. F. Hutton-like; "I really don't think any of this is necessary") is conveniently absent even though we know what he doesn't want. You can stop laughing anytime now—this was a serious work-and-witness trip. There was a lot on the line....

Painting textured walls is interesting; it's amazing how you can think it covered when it didn't especially if the lighting is weak. When you're in a hurry, I suggest poor lighting. But when it really matters, I suggest a three-hundred-watt halogen lamp acting like a heat lamp on your baldhead, while painting your mother-in-law's house. Just so you know, Betty is proud!

The Journey calls us to give a loyal, pupil to seeker representation of what it means to be a follower of Jesus, often referred to as a *Christian,* or in Scripture a *disciple.* What impact does an active adherent of Jesus' teachings have on our world today? Let's take a look. Will you ask God, our Father: *"What would You like to say to me today?"*

FROM THE FATHER'S HEART

What does salt do? It brings out the flavor of whatever it seasons. That's why you are here as a disciple of Jesus—to bring out the reality of My Presence, the God-flavors of life on earth.

What does light do? It makes what was hidden able to be seen. That's why you are here as a disciple of Jesus—to bring out the reality of My presence in the world I've created.

Flavor is present; colors are everywhere, just as I am. I'm no secret, not really. Jesus made Me clear to those who taste and see. Jesus, the Life-light, blazed out of My Presence to make Me known, and the darkness could not put out the True Light.

As a true disciple you are re-made to be your true self; your child-of-God self. This is accomplished by your simple, faith act of believing Jesus is who He claimed to be and is revealed to be in Scripture.

It's not like I'm some well-kept secret, hidden away—I am everywhere. You know it. So, salt your world with an authentic representation of Jesus. Light your world with a consistent reflection of Jesus.

You believe and make a difference by open house living. Open-life living with others will bring the hunger and thirst for Me—salt. Reflective-living with others will help them see in the dark and discover the way—light.

Some walk in the counsel of the wicked, some stand in the way of the rebellious, and some sit in the seat of know-it-alls, mocking. But you are blessed, for you desire and seek out My instruction consistently. You have chosen the fruitful path, like a tree planted by streams of water. No matter what, you are graced to remain steady; not so are the wicked, which are like chaff blown away by the wind. I chart the road you take. Aligned with Me and My ways, whatever you do prospers. Rejoice and be glad.

You belong to Christ, as true disciples do. Everything connected with getting your own way and mindlessly responding to what the world says is necessary is crucified, killed-off. The Journey is about your life being consistent with your relationship with Me through Jesus. You are one who believes in Jesus, The Journey is about learning to know Me and My ways more deeply and helping others learn of Me and My ways with no pretense, just authentic living it out day in, day out—no matter what!

Salt brings out the flavor already present. Light brings out the color already present. Bring out the flavor and color of life by exercising your faith in Me, and I will work through you. I'm counting on you to be a true disciple—no games, just real living in your world, as My child.

I love you,
Abba

YOUR HEART

In your quiet time with God, ask Him this question: "Father, what would You like to say to me today?" Write what you believe He is saying to you. Write your name, and begin to capture whatever comes to mind, just as if God were speaking to you. For you see, He is ...

Now, take a moment to write your thoughts to our Father.

Here are a few questions to help you reflect on true discipleship:

- How "salty" is your life to those around you?

- How is your relationship with the Father, through Jesus, impacting your everyday, ordinary life?

- What "flavor" and "color" is your life bringing to others?

Prayer

Father, I thank You for the people who have been salt and light in my journey. My desire is to be a consistent representative of Your kingdom, salt and light to those who know You but are tested, those who are seeking You and almost there, and those who are just awaking to their lost state. Thank You for Jesus, my Savior open doors for me to share the Good News of our Master. For the glory of Your name, amen

Week 42

RECONCILIATION

Devotional Scriptures

2 Corinthians 5:14–21
Romans 5:1–11
John 14:22–31
Philippians 4:2–9
Acts 10:34–43
Luke 6:37–42

The Psalmist's Pen

Psalm 130, Psalm 84

FROM STEVE'S HEART

This past month will forever be remembered in my journey as "September Happens." Forgive me as I recount just the peaks and valleys that felt like Trail Ridge Road in Colorado's Rocky Mountain National Park.

> Saturday the 1st—my position suddenly ends, eliminated due to budget cuts
>
> Tuesday the 4th—we send Monica & Kalen off to Mexico to visit Severiano; the saga continues of trying to work with American Immigration; paperwork issues continue into seventeen months; it is my fifty-third birthday

Wednesday the 5th—Max Steven is born; our sixth grandchild

Thursday the 6th—Max is transferred to Baptist Memorial Hospital, NICU; it is his brother Nolan's fourth birthday

Friday the 7th—Rita's birthday; we remained in OKC to help Jeffrey, Stephanie and the kids

Monday the 10th—return home for Farewell Lunch with some friends from work; Rita picked up stomach virus from Nolan and is not feeling well; but Max is released to go home from the hospital!

Wednesday the 12th—a low-key celebration of our thirty-first wedding anniversary

Thursday the 20th—trip to Kansas to visit our parents in Neodesha and Independence; roots revisited and did a little fix-it work, another family oriented work-and-witness trip

Wednesday the 26th—Immigration notifies us; Severiano's waver is "denied"

Thursday the 27th—Jeffrey called; Stephanie is experiencing post-partum blues

Friday the 28th—attend funeral for former employee's two-year-old son; he drown in their pool; we head to Edmond to help Jeffrey and Stephanie during this unplanned, difficult transition following Max's birth

Saturday the 29th—back home in Tulsa, restless night

Sunday the 30th—preaching at a local church; *"What would You like to say to us, Father?"* That local fellowship gave us a love offering, which was the exact amount needed to cover Monica's airfare to Mexico. God honored our faith and met a need. It was a significant sign of God's work behind the scenes *and* encouragement for Rita, my weary, traveling companion of thirty-one years.

The Journey includes Septembers, and you have your story. Now, I've recounted part of mine. Your September could have greater peaks and valleys! My point is not to compare stories. It is to illustrate that life happens and to remind us that when September happens, God is here or there to help us reconcile life. Said another way, He helps us make peace with life.

Will you ask God, our Father: "*What would You like to say to me today?*"

FROM THE FATHER'S HEART

You are blessed, for your strength is in Me, and your heart is set on The Journey; on seeking My face and My ways on your pilgrimage. As your path descends through the Valley of Baca—the valley of tears, a time of weeping, a lonesome valley, you will discover cool springs flowing with autumn blessings. You will go from strength to strength traveling paths that leads to the last turn; we will stand face-to-face. Travel on; make Me the strength of your life. I am your sun—light and life—your shield and protection. I bestow favor and honor; no good thing will I withhold from you on The Journey. You are blessed for you trust in Me.

Making peace with life starts as you make peace with Me. Reconciliation begins with an acknowledgement of separation accompanied by crying out for mercy. An awareness of your wrong doings, of how crazy it would be if I kept a record of your sins, will jolt you into reality—Who could stand? Know this; it is my default setting to forgive. Those who get it, worship Me, rejoicing in forgiveness sought and given.

As you wait for Me to act on your behalf, put your hope in Me. Place your life on the line with Me, as you watch and wait—as I come, so does My love; as I come, so does reconciliation and redemption.

Reconciliation is about relationship—getting back together; your relationship with Me, your relationship with others, and their relationship with Me. No one moves toward establishing friendship with Me until they reconcile their need for reconciliation. Every person must exercise the gift of faith I initially give, so you may believe in Me. That leads to your desire to be pleasing to Me. Then you understand: there is coming a day when everyone will appear before Christ to take what's coming as a result of your actions, either good or bad. No small thing.

Reconciliation is My work on your behalf through Jesus Christ, the Messiah. You must believe that one man, Jesus Christ, My Son, died for every one person. Why is this big deal? So you will no longer live for yourself, but for Him who died for you and was raised again. Reconciled, you will enjoy a far better life than if left to your own ways. Reconciliation is a fresh start provided by Jesus … a restored relationship with Me. With the forgiveness of your sins, this separation has been taken care of by the Messiah.

You must make peace with Me before you can make peace with life. And what is peace? It's not merely absence of trouble; peace is everything that makes for your highest good, life as it is meant to be. Of course, you must understand and define life correctly to pursue life as it is meant to be or peace is not even an option. Scripture reveals to you what this looks like. Jesus' life reveals what this looks like. The world's outlook on what makes for your highest good is self-centered for the most part. Transformation into Christ-likeness is how your life is meant to be lived. Reconciliation, entering into a personal, faith-based relationship with Me through Jesus, is the place to begin if you want to make peace with life.

Reconciliation with Me leads to making peace with others. As one reconciled you are invited to participate in the ministry of reconciliation. In light of pending "judgment day" you are to be vigilant in your effort to persuade others to be reconciled with Me. To do this you must work from a focused perspective: Jesus died for everyone. Sympathy, compassion, and a burden for others will not support you in this hard work. Only your personal experience of My love for you will sustain this ministry of reconciliation.

Reconciliation, making peace with life, requires you first make peace with Me, so I can give you a fresh start. Then, the ministry of reconciliation comes, making peace with others and guiding them to make peace with Me. Can I count on you, My friend?

I love you,
Abba

YOUR HEART

In your quiet time with God, ask Him this question: "Father, what would You like to say to me today?" Write what you believe He is saying to you. Write your name, and begin to capture whatever comes to mind, just as if God were speaking to you. For you see, He is …

Here are a few questions to help as you reflect upon reconciliation:

- Have you had or are you having your September?

- What role does being at peace with God relationally play in being at peace today, no matter what?

- Who needs the ministry of reconciliation in your world? What will you do?

Now, take a moment to write your thoughts to our Father.

Prayer

Father, thank You for giving me faith to believe in Jesus as my personal Savior and for the fresh start. Thank You for the message and ministry of reconciliation for all of my people relationships; help me see life from Your perspective, so I remain vigilant with the Gospel. Thank You for Your Son, Jesus, who died for my sins. Here is my life; take all of me. For the glory of Your name, amen

Week 43

UNLIMITED GRACE

Devotional Scriptures

Colossians 2:8–15
Ephesians 2:1–10
Romans 6:1–14
Romans 8:1–11
2 Timothy 2:1–13
John 8:1–11

The Psalmist's Pen

Psalm 141

FROM STEVE'S HEART

Over twenty years ago, I had my first major experience of "life happens." I was the pastor of a small church in rural Oklahoma. It was my first church as "senior pastor" following several years of associate ministry in youth and music. Things were going ... along.

Let me back up. Within six months of my arrival, they asked the presiding district leader for a replacement. It was a small church in a small town in a section of the state where folks truly felt abandoned—it was the panhandle of Oklahoma. (Look at the map if you can't immediately figure this one out; who was responsible for setting those boundaries?) Anyway, my youthful zeal and inexperience probably rubbed them the wrong way.

So, at their request, I resigned; I changed my approach and sure enough, another six months passed. They wanted me to *stay* as pastor. Over the months ahead, we reached out to several young couples needing direction in life. Fred and Mary were such a couple.

I remember one week in particular. Fred came to Sunday morning worship and found his seat in the sanctuary before he realized he forgot to put out his cigarette. His boot and pant cuff became his ash tray! We laughed later as he related the story. He was an oil field guy getting to know God and learning how to accept help with his life, his marriage to Mary, his role as dad, and with his cocaine addiction.

Grace was offered by God, but apparently not everyone could handle it. At the end of three years a majority of the congregation said it was time for me to move on. A *hard left* on what I thought was a *straight road* on The Journey. What happened next? God's healing grace and mercy touched our lives as He opened a new assignment ... at just the right time.

The Journey reminds us that God's grace is unlimited—*I am so grateful!* Whatever you are facing, do you believe God's grace is unlimited? That He will help you navigate the hard left turns along life's road.

Ask God, our Father: "*What would You like to say to me today?*"

FROM THE FATHER'S HEART

You are My workmanship. This means I exercised my God capabilities and creative powers to fashion you. Not just your personality, talents, gifts, and physical stature, but also the purpose of your life. You are the result of My labor.

My hands created you to join Me in the work I do, to be My apprentice. By the way, this was no afterthought—the work I have in mind for you has been waiting for some time and for this exact moment. How do you merit such favor? What have you done that is so amazing that I would want you to join Me and My kingdom work?

Nothing.

This is all about My gift of grace.

Now, back to the beginning. Jesus is My "corporate head-hunter," if you will. When He found you, it was not that you were ready, but that you had potential. Actually, you were bogged down in that old stagnant life of sin. The world, which is clueless about living, was telling you how to live, and you were buying it. Unbelief, disobedience, doing what you felt like doing, when you felt like doing it—you were going your own way. Pretty disappointing for Me, but not shocking. You know, if it had been left up to man, and you were managing you, you would have lost your cool and done away with the whole thing—including yourself.

But that's not who I am. With My immense mercy and incredible love, I embraced you. I took your old, sin-dead life and made you alive in Christ. Taking the initiative, I chose you, lifted you off death row in order that you may join Jesus.

Think about it; I rescued you from death. Then I released My grace and kindness, which will continue through all eternity—My gift. Jesus, the headhunter, found and qualified you to be My apprentice; all that was required was for you to believe it.

Why is it like this? Frankly, if you had any part in this you'd be tempted to brag about how you landed this position with Me. Facts are, you did not create yourself nor can you save yourself. I am Creator God, your Redeemer in Jesus Christ. That is My unlimited grace for you … the desire and ability to respond to all this, to Me. With this clear, now you can go to work for Me. Once again My grace allows you to carry out your role—My unlimited grace!

Unlimited grace means not only will I forgive your sins when you place your faith in Jesus, but I will free you from the bondage of sin. To help you understand this let's think about baptism. Baptism is a powerful image. When lowered into the water, it's like you have been buried with Jesus in His death. When raised up out of the baptismal water, it's like you have been raised with Jesus in His resurrection.

Grace brought you to own your sins, confess, and receive forgiveness. Grace brings you to the point of life where you are raised into a light-filled life, a fresh start. By My grace you are included in Christ's sin-conquering death and included in Christ's life-saving resurrection. You've been raised from the dead, so live like it. Imagine the impact on how you would live if you nearly died but somehow survived. How might your daily life be impacted?

Transformation into Christ-likeness is not about trying harder to live by a set of rules; it is embracing what My Holy Spirit is doing in you as a person alive in Christ! Just trying harder to be like Jesus out of your own efforts leads down a wrong path; you'll end up self-righteous and self-absorbed. Tapping into My unlimited grace allows you to trust Me to work in your life. Pay attention to My Word, Jesus, and His example and you will receive an ever-growing desire and ability to be pleasing to Me. You will find the spacious place of My grace. Anyone completely absorbed in self, ignores Me; if you think more about self than Me ... *that* limits My grace.

But when I reside in your life, you'll find it pretty hard to ignore Me (although that is an option). Welcome Me and you will understand this and you will experience life as it is meant to be. What I did for Jesus—raising Him from the dead—I will do for you; bringing you alive unto Me. My unlimited grace gives you life so you may give Me your life, all because I love you, and you now love Me.

My unlimited grace is not just about forgiveness of sins and freedom from sin's bondage. Grace, the desire and ability I give so you can live pleasing to Me, impacts The Journey. Whether The Journey brings you to a season of testing or joyous blessing, to a point of failure or unwavering obedience in relationships, your purpose, disappointments, plans, your gifting or your life lived as My child. As oxygen is free and present to support your body, so My grace is free and present to support your fresh start, life in Christ.

I love you,
Abba

YOUR HEART

In your quiet time with God, ask Him this question: "Father, what would You like to say to me today?" Write what you believe He is saying to you. Write your name, and begin to capture whatever comes to mind, just as if God were speaking to you. For you see, He is …

Now, take a moment to write your thoughts to our Father.

Here are a few questions to help you reflect on God's unlimited grace:

- When you are thinking of being Jesus' apprentice what comes to mind?

- What are your thoughts on water baptism?

- How does being pre-occupied about yourself limit God's grace?

Prayer

Thank You, Father, for Your amazing, unlimited grace. I come to once again place myself in the path of Your rushing love and limitless compassion. Help me be a channel of Your grace to those who need both the desire and ability to live pleasing to You. I am so thankful for Your grace toward me, Hallelujah! For the glory of Your name, amen

Week 44

RELIABLE STEWARDS

Devotional Scriptures

1 Corinthians 4:1–13
1 Thessalonians 1:1–10
2 Thessalonians 1:1–4
Luke 12:35–48
1 Timothy 2:4–6
Revelations 22:1–12

The Psalmist's Pen

Psalm 24, Psalm 50

FROM STEVE'S HEART

So you're on The Journey with me; I'm six weeks into this "transition." Last week, it seemed important to get our growing family together for a couple of days; Monica had returned from Mexico, Max was a month old, one aunt and uncle had yet to meet him, and there was a lot of life going on in our family. So, we enjoyed several days of "full house"—six under the age of six; thankfully they brought their parents. Someone was with us over the course of five days. It was exhausting, but it was a good thing and the helpful thing to do.

Just to keep things interesting a twenty-four hour virus started working its way through the ranks Saturday night; it came knocking on my door Tuesday after everyone returned home. To say I was drained would be appropriate. My ability to hear this week's Scriptures on the theme of living as stewards was difficult.

Late Tuesday afternoon, I wrote in my Journal…

Abba, I feel more confused today than last week. Dream Giver, Master, Savior, King of my life, Lord God Almighty––wow! Thank you that I'm feeling better…for this beautiful day. I feel more uncertain and clueless today than a week ago, but I accept this "sick day" like a rainy day while building the pond…a "time-out" by Your decree and providence. You are My God, keep me moving forward in this transition as I wait and rest in You; obedient and responsible, too.

Wednesday morning's journal entry reads…

Good morning, Father…it's good to know, that You know, because I am still "searching matters out." You are God, I am not—I embrace that. Here I am; where are we going? I do not know. You are my Shepherd, I am Your sheep…lead me to green pastures and quiet waters; restore my soul. Guide me in righteousness; the right path for Your glory. Surely goodness and love will follow me all the days of my life…I will dwell in Your presence. Please release Your Spirit to bring me counsel, comfort, discernment, and power to press through.

It felt like I just licked my finger and was sticking it in the air to see which way the wind was blowing. After a little inventory was taken; I continued to journal…

+ 1978–1995 / 20 years of local church ministry experience

+ 1997–2007 / 10 years of business, sales, sales management experience

+ Education…Bachelor of Arts, Master of Ministry

+ Product development and training expertise-Battle Plan for Believers Ministries, Inc.

+ Communication Skills, both oral and written, are strong

+ Thirty-one years of marriage, 3 daughters, and sons-in-law, and 6 grandchildren

I'm to be a steward of this. So I'm asking You, Giver of my life, talent, gifting, my journey...my Lord and Savior, Master...what would glorify You?

Last week one of my job applications was dismissed, "Looking for someone more in line with the position." Then, another door closed. More conversations with the advisors I'm tapping into...some of the fog lifts; waiting, resting, trusting...*encouraged by our Father.*

Friday, no progress on this week's writing, but God did have a chat with me about fear...fear is *exaggeration of the danger ahead.* There was more, just no space to share it here. There are options—ideas are running pretty wide.

The question for all of us to consider: "*What does it mean to be a reliable steward?*"

Here is what I received, will you ask God, our Father: "*What would You like to say to me today?*"

FROM THE FATHER'S HEART

The earth is mine, as is everything in it, the world, and all who live in it, for I pushed back the waters to let dry ground appear. Listen, for I am God.

In the days of old, do you think it was the sacrifice of bulls and goats that I really was after? I had no need of them. Every animal of the forest, every animal of the field, and the birds upon the mountains are all mine. It wasn't about hunger; the world and everything in it is mine. No, I didn't need their sacrifices to feed myself!

What I do desire is your true thanks for what I offer you, for you to fulfill your promises made. I want you to trust Me in your troubled-times so I can rescue you. Then, raise your voice to give Me glory and honor as a witness to others of My faithfulness.

All creation, including your life rightfully belongs to Me; you are invited to be a steward. You were created in Our image. In the beginning I blessed Adam and Eve, released them to multiply; to fill the earth, subdue it, to rule over all birds, fish, and animals—to enjoy seed bearing plants and fruit trees. Everything I had created was excellent in everyway.

What was My plan? Man was to be a reliable steward. But with the fall of Adam, his disobedience corrupted the human nature. Man mistakenly positioned himself as god…and still does. I am God and you are not. However, you are called to be a steward to manage My grand idea of creation and humanity. You are to be loyal, dependable, and trustworthy, ready—a servant in My kingdom and in the world.

Your stewardship responsibilities cover creation, the environment as you refer to it today. This is true. But this world will be destroyed and there will be a new one—it is My plan.

The greater call is personal stewardship. It is about your life and your response to My love, My forgiveness, My authority. The Journey calls you to be a reliable steward. You must first acknowledge Who I am and who you are. I am the Creator, you are the created…Master, bond slave…Shepherd, lost sheep…Redeemer, the redeemed…Righteous, unrighteous, but made right in My sight through Christ. It's all about understanding our relationship. You were separated, rebellious, dead in your sins but I made you alive in Christ My gift of love.

What response do I desire? Your true thanks and your promise kept; that you would call upon Me in trouble, so I may answer you and bring glory to My name. I want you to be a reliable steward of the Gospel. Be faithful with the Message; how My heart longs for all men to be saved, to understand I am God, the one true God; there is only one Mediator, Christ Jesus.

The Journey is about being a reliable steward of your life, your new life in Christ, and the message. When the Message came to you it wasn't just words—something happened in you. I want your continued cooperation so My transforming power is free to work. Yes, even in the difficult times ... listen for My voice, receive My joy, and so honor Me.

Let the headline declare: you are Mine. Let your life lived out before others be the message. Your ambition is to be pleasing to Me in Christ Jesus. A Reliable Steward manages life's "stuff" which includes experiences, successes, and failures, My gifts, your talent, and personality, your victories and defeats—all that makes you who you are; live to My honor and glory.

How will you remain dependable, loyal, trustworthy, and reliable? Remember the promise of Jesus. He is coming again and will make all things plain that are hidden and set all things right. Yes, He will show up and bring His payroll, too. You will be paid in full for your life's work as My reliable steward.

I love you,
Abba

YOUR HEART

In your quiet time with God, ask Him this question: "Father, what would You like to say to me today?" Write what you believe He is saying to you. Write your name, and begin to capture whatever comes to mind, just as if God were speaking to you. For you see, He is ...

Now, take a moment to write your thoughts to our Father.

Here are a few questions to help you reflect on being a reliable steward:

- Why do you think Abba puts such a high value on a spirit of gratitude and giving thanks?

- How is personal stewardship being lived out on your journey?

- What would need to change for you to be a reliable steward?

Prayer

Thank You, Father, for Your investment in my life. You are my Shepherd, God Almighty; I am Your child resting, trusting eager to honor You. Grant me the grace to manage the resources of this world, faithfully share the Good News of the Gospel and live my life for Your kingdom. Here am I, Your willing servant. I am so thankful that You trust me, oh that I would be found worthy... In the name of our Savior and Lord, Jesus, amen.

Week 45

IT'S POSSIBLE

Devotional Scriptures

Exodus 3:7–22
Jeremiah 32:16–24
Isaiah 40:18–31
Romans 4:13–25, 5:1–11
Acts 12:1–17
Hebrews 1:1–14

The Psalmist's Pen

Psalm 103

FROM STEVE'S HEART

What seems impossible to you today?

Perhaps a better question: what matters of concern do you face that need a God-solution? That's the catch isn't it—we want the thing done now, according to our expectations, and as often as not think we can get it done. Wow, what a limiting response to life's challenges!

Think about God's response to our biggest human need—establishing a right relationship with Him. First, motivated by love for us, Jesus died for our sins … raising us from the dead spiritually to being alive unto God and in right standing with Him. Then, He sent His Holy Spirit to purify, comfort, counsel, and guide our daily lives. He accomplished all this while remaining true to His law, His character, and our nature as human beings. Yes, it's a big deal.

That being the case, what about those other matters of concern in your life and mine? All things are possible! Whether an unexpected career transition. Or a disappointing "Denied" stamped on immigration paperwork, keeping a young family separated, and requiring further appeals.

Or what is it that rocks your world today? The Journey calls us as followers of Jesus to believe in Him and know that all things are possible. How do we move forward when we're waiting for what seems impossible to become a done deal?

Here is what I received, will you ask God, our Father: "*What would You like to say to me today?*"

FROM THE FATHER'S HEART

The forgiveness of your sins—the healing of life's diseases, redemption from the pit and setbacks, and the pouring out of My love and compassion on you? Will you praise My name as you remember that I satisfy your desires with good things and renew your strength for another day and recall My response of compassion and grace, removing your sins as far as the east is from the west? Will you praise My name as you meditate on the magnitude of My love for those who fear Me?

Is it possible that a bush would burn without burning up? But even greater—is it possible that I would see the misery of My people, hear them groaning and crying out because of their bondage, and be concerned to the point of coming down to rescue them, and so raise up a leader to make possible their deliverance from an oppressive earthly king?

Am I the Sovereign Lord who made the heavens and the earth by My great power and outstretched arm—is there anything too hard for Me? Yes, even the promise that I will be your God; give you singleness of heart and action so you will always fear Me for your own good and the good of those who come after you. All things are possible, indeed.

What then is the basis of this saying, "All things are possible?" How does it come down to your world and impact your life? Let's look and see, considering Abraham as our case study.

The famous promise to Abraham that he would be the father of many nations originated with Me. It was My decision *to speak* this promise, it was Abraham's decision *to enter* into the moment and believe. All things are possible that begin with My promise.

Fulfillment of My promise depends on a couple of things. First, you must totally trust Me, My ways, and then embrace Me—what I do and how I do things. You see My promise is a gift to you. This is about your faith in Me and My promise(s).

Abraham dared to trust Me to do what only I could do. In his situation, it was to give life to the dead and call things that are not as though they were, i.e.—make something out of next to nothing. When everything appeared hopeless, Abraham believed. He made a choice to live life, not on the basis of what he saw he couldn't do, but on the basis of what I said I would do. This allowed Me to fulfill the promise. All things are possible!

Can you imagine the impact on Abraham's thinking, outlook, and faith if he would have focused on his century-old body and the painful decades of Sarah's infertility? "It's hopeless," would have been the only logical perspective with such a focus. What did he do? He did not allow unbelief to knock him off his feet, turning into cautious skepticism regarding My promise. Instead he took hold of My promise, which strengthened his faith, and by My grace, stood strong. He was fully persuaded that I had power to do what I promised.

That's why I declared Abraham righteous—he trusted Me to set him right in My sight. This is the foundation for you, too. You are righteous in My sight when you believe that I brought Jesus to life even when things appeared hopeless. You are righteous in My sight when you accept the reality that Jesus' sacrifice was for your sins, just as I promised.

It begins with My promise regarding the gift of life through Jesus' death and resurrection. It ends with My promise of Jesus' return for His own. That is the big picture regarding all things are possible—My salvation plan. Now, let's bring it down to your big picture, where each and every aspect of your life is lived.

Again, it starts with My promise. The promise comes from Me to you. Remember, My promise will never violate Scripture or My character. So to hear My promise accurately you must know Me. My Word, wisdom, and godly counsel are available to you—all guided by My Holy Spirit.

The fulfillment of My promise requires total trust. Will you trust Me with your "impossible situation"? The fulfillment of My promise requires total surrender. Will you embrace My ways and timing with your "impossible situation"? My promise is a gift to be received by faith.

When it appears hopeless … believe anyway.

Key lesson: power is given to whomever or whatever you focus on, so watch where you fix your focus. Will it be "a century old body" or My promise? If you focus on *what if* or the mountain of obstacles your faith will be shaken. When you focus on Who I am, My faithfulness, power, love, mercy, and My Word, you will strengthen your faith and you will see that all things are possible!

How do you keep holding on while waiting for My promise to be delivered? Is there help for the long waits? Consider Peter's story. The ruler of his day wrongfully placed Peter in jail with plans to kill him in a few days. Peter was so confident in Me that he slept like a baby. That's right, while under heavy guard and shackled to two guards he slept.

What else was happening behind the scenes? What else was going on … ? Followers of Jesus joined together in prayer for Peter's release. Yes, when waiting for My promise, it helps to have praying friends. In the tough times you need a support system of others standing in the gap. Will you enlist followers of Jesus to stand in the gap for you? And if you are in the season of blessing will you stand in the gap for others? If so, you will be strengthened to see that all things are possible.

Enjoy your journey to My promise fulfilled.

I love you,
Abba

YOUR HEART

In your quiet time with God, ask Him this question: "Father, what would You like to say to me today?" Write what you believe He is saying to you. Write your name, and begin to capture whatever comes to mind, just as if God were speaking to you. For you see, He is...

Now, take a moment to write your thoughts to our Father.

Here are a few questions to help you reflect on limitless possibilities:

- How does the role of praising God fit into your journey?

- Have you ever faced anything in life that seemed too hard for God? What was it? When was it? Where were you along The Journey? What happened?

- How do you hold on while waiting for an answer?

Prayer

Thank You, Father, for knowing me, my life situation, and exactly what I need. Thank You for caring about me ... for Your promise of salvation, but also Your promise to be with me in all things relating to my every day, ordinary life. This situation (you name it) I commit to You and totally trust You to work things out to the glory of Your name. Thank You for those who stand with me in prayer ... help me be faithful in lifting others in their time of need, too. In the name of our Savior and Lord, Jesus, amen.

FAITHFUL AND OBEDIENT

Devotional Scriptures

Hebrews 11:1–16
Acts 8:1–8
Acts 11:19–26
Matthew 21:28–32
Luke 12:35–48
Luke 17:1–10

The Psalmist's Pen

Psalm 92

FROM STEVE'S HEART

Yesterday was *not* one of my most noteworthy days—low productivity, a bit challenging, not one of those days you brag about as a professional human being. It was a work-in-progress day, if you know what I mean. In fact, this week I had more of those moments than I care to claim.

The answer to "What's next, Father?" continues to lead to a coaching practice. Lord willing, I will help individuals get to the next level in their life. The objective is to lead someone through a process whereby they understand what got them *here* (their current level of leadership) will not get them *there* (reaching their full potential with expanded influence). The process is designed to help someone see what they cannot see—the stuff others encounter when working with them. Then, help them chart a course that brings change and more effective behavior. Simply put, my mission is to help successful people with a desire for personal growth and professional development, to make the journey from *here* to *there*.

Now, back to a week filled with underwhelming moments. Tuesday I began reading the textbook on preparation for executive coaching training, which begins Monday. Here is an excerpt from my Journal for Tuesday.

> Flipping through the book I became a little discouraged with the forms in the Appendix. Questions and doubts came at me...yes, there is a significant financial investment going into this. The Sherpa Guide is a process-driven executive coaching approach. It's very detailed, specific and narrow in scope; no turning back now.

Then, I believe our Father said to me:

> Steve, relax...receive this as a resource and starting place; you will find your way, style and approach as always. Do not fear. Notice the Dedication statement by the authors; what you did not know is this—Brenda Corbet and Judith Colemon are Mine, too. Read their dedication statement...they wrote:

"We are in awe of how God orchestrates things. We are clear that He places people in our lives just at the appointed time to fulfill His purpose."

Any questions...?

None that seem appropriate here in Your holy presence.

Then live and stay in the shadow of My wings, let Me be your Refuge...yes, your Rock...even God Almighty, your Coach.

Thank You...You are faithful, I pursue obedience.

> This week I was surprised by the play on words of our theme, *faithful* and *obedient*. Here is what I received. Will you ask God, "*What would You like to say to me today?*"

FROM THE FATHER'S HEART

As you begin your day, remember My love and give expression of gratitude.

At the end of your day rehearse My faithfulness and take heart.

Consider all I have done for you so you may experience the strength that comes from My joy. Consider everything I have done––the works of My hands and the depth of My ways will help keep you from foolish thinking. People who do not reflect on My love and faithfulness don't get it—they don't understand that temporal success cannot deliver them from misery and judgment—that I am God and they are not.

Those who resist and oppose My authority and reject My love will be destroyed. Those who are obedient will flourish in My care and ultimately be in My presence forever. Enjoy the shelter of My love. Let your life of obedience honor Me, as you are an exhibit of My faithful care and abundant goodness.

I am faithful; you are to be obedient and in your obedience you will be faithful. Yet, there is an aspect of being faithful that belongs to you—exercising faith. I am firmly and devotedly supportive of you. I am consistently consistent with truth—faithful. You are free to believe in Me and trust Me. You have faith—thus, faithful. My faithfulness comes from who I am. Your faithfulness comes from having faith, believing in, and trusting Me. This faith is the firm foundation under everything that makes your life worth living. The fundamental fact of existence is based upon your trusting My trust-worthiness. Your faith gives you a handle on what you cannot see and hope.

For example, you see the universe created at My command. What you see, the world you live in, created by what or who you cannot see—Me. I am faithful; you are to have faith. Why is this so important? Anyone who comes to Me and desires to please Me has to believe two things: 1) that I exist, and 2) that I care about you so much that I respond to your seeking Me.

Your obedience follows faith. Your ability and willingness to obey requires faith. Faithfulness on your part requires faith that leads you to seek Me, to listen and to submit to My authority. I am faithful; you are to be obedient. Life is worth living. Your faith is in Jesus—the Way, the Truth, and the Life. Your faith is in My Jesus-Revelation—Son of God, Son of Man.

I want you to be sure of what you hope for—eternal life. To be certain of what you do not see—My kingdom, Sovereignty, and Authority the sure foundation for your life. I love you. I am proud of you as one who seeks My face, accepts and follows Jesus, and whose life ambition is to be pleasing to Me. [Your name], I love you.

Go forward confident in My love and faithfulness, My peace will guard your heart and mind as you, like Abraham are "going without knowing." When called, he obeyed and went to a place promised. Faithful, I am obedient; you are to be. It is The Journey.

The Journey is about *exercising* faith, not having more per se. You either trust Me right now or you do not trust Me right now. It's not about having more faith so you can trust Me more. The question is this: Will you allow your confidence in Me and My devoted support to impact you right now? Will your faith in My trustworthiness liberate you to obey, to carry out My wishes, and to yield to My authority? Faith is the fundamental fact of your existence—you either trust Me or not; everything that makes life make sense rests on this foundation.

It's yes or no, not more or less. Do you believe I exist? Do you believe I respond to your seeking Me? Do you believe I love you? Do you believe that it takes faith to be pleasing to Me? Are you sure of what you hope for and certain of what you do not see? It's yes or no, not more or less.

Growth in faith concerns your ability to live by faith, not have more faith. Faced with life's challenges, disappointment, temptation, choices, setbacks, how you will respond? That is where "more faith" comes in.

Tonight, as you lay down will you say "I listened and obeyed

more today than yesterday"? That is The Journey of faithfulness and obedience.

I love you,
Abba

YOUR HEART

In your quiet time with God, ask Him this question: "Father, what would You like to say to me today?" Write what you believe He is saying to you. Write your name, and begin to capture whatever comes to mind, just as if God were speaking to you. For you see, He is...

Now, take a moment to write your thoughts to our Father.

Here are a few questions and suggestions to help you as you reflect upon the getting there:

- When you think of faithful and obedient, what first comes to mind?

- How does your view of God impact your desire to be faithful and obedient?

- If you truly believe God is faithful what might you step out and pursue?

Prayer

Father, I rejoice in You and praise You; great is Your faithfulness! Grant me grace to listen, and obey, and demonstrate my faith in You. I stand in awe of how You orchestrate things demonstrating Your love and compassion towards me. Help me develop a consistent response of obedience knowing You are faithful and thus placing my faith in You in all things. In the name of our Savior and Lord, Jesus, amen

Week 47

LIVING AS A SERVANT

Devotional Scriptures

John 13:1–11
Romans 15:1–13
2 Corinthians 6:1–10
2 Corinthians 4:1–17
2 Corinthians 7:1–13
Matthew 10:24–39

The Psalmist's Pen

Psalm 71

FROM STEVE'S HEART

It was late Friday afternoon when I arrived at Oklahoma City's Will Rogers International Airport returning from a week in Dallas and still had a two-hour drive home to Tulsa. My daughters had extended an invitation to dinner; I declined thinking it would be good just to get home. But when the second invitation came, I recognized the value and gladly accepted. *I don't always get things the first time.*

Just that week I went through a values clarification exercise as part of my executive coaching certification program. We act on our values everyday; the exercise is powerful and can bring insight. Which was my experience: I recognized a gap between one of my stated values and my behavior. A little painful to admit, but I'm thankful for the reality check.

While the girls finished preparing dinner, I went outside to be affectionately mobbed by the grandchildren playing in the back yard. Six-year-old Maggie had her roller skates on and was walk-skating in the grass. Seizing the moment, I turned into her skating coach; yes, I can…or did roller skate as a teenager!

Immediately after dinner, Maggie asked if we could go back outside for more skating. A time to start was negotiated, and she patiently sat on my lap during a little after dinner adult visit until the appointed time. We worked on technique as she hung onto my arms, and I walked backwards in front of her chanting instructions.

My next departure time approached. Maggie asked if I wanted to play a game. My body and mind was ready to hit the road and get home. But, the moment presented me a probing question: "What did I value?" It's not that I couldn't say no to that persistent little girl with her loving petition, I have before; but this *servanthood* idea was moving on my heart and the recent value-gap exercise was impacting my ability to say "no"; I chose to say, "Yes, let's play."

Although we use *servanthood* in conversation around the church, it is not found in the dictionary. A person who practices living as a servant appears to be an appropriate definition.

You know what is interesting about Friday night's experience? I enjoyed dinner with a few of my children and grandchildren. We connected for a little bit, made a memory and the game only lasted *ten* minutes! Everyone appeared satisfied.

What is interesting is this: when we serve others, we are served something unexpected in return—must be a God-thing.

Here is what I received. Will you ask God: "*What would You like to say to me today?*"

FROM THE FATHER'S HEART

Jesus knew who He was, where He came from, and where He was headed. This freed Him to serve. He got up from the table and washed the disciple's feet. The Twelve did not recognize the need or opportunity. Servanthood requires knowing who you are before you can be free to serve—free from a self-centered approach to life and people.

You may not always understand in the moment what is going on, much like Peter when Jesus washed his feet. But it is the washing that allows you to be a part of what I am doing. Of course this is the washing away of your sins; it is about holiness (belonging to Me) not hygiene. The feet washing by Jesus demonstrated servanthood, and as you serve others, you will live a blessed life.

As a believer strong in the faith, you need to step up and lend a hand to those who may falter and not just when convenient. Strength is for service, not status. You are to look after the good of the people I place around you—just ask yourself, "How might I help them?" Yes, this is about exercising talent, gifts, and skills to make a difference just like Jesus.

Did Jesus avoid people with trouble? Do I go with you through times of trouble? Yes, I come alongside to help you out. Now hear My calling and receive the counsel of Scripture, let it characterize your life keeping you alert for whatever I will do next and how I may invite your participation.

Come, let Me—the God of living hope—fill you up with joy and with My peace. Then your believing life will be filled with My Spirit's life-giving energy, all spilling over with hope!

Your ministry opportunity is a direct result of My mercy, so don't lose heart when you run into opposition or hard times. As My Servant, stay faithful to the truth then people must deal with Me, not you, or your presentation.

The real problem is twofold: 1) people are looking in the wrong place, and 2) going the wrong direction. This keeps them from seriously thinking about Me. Caught up in the world they can see, they don't work on believing what they can't see. The god of this age has blinded their minds with unbelief and deception so they cannot see Jesus, the best picture of Me you'll see in this life.

Remember the message is not about you—it's all about Jesus.

Deliver the Good News; demonstrate a life filled with light as one who knows Jesus. People will miss the brightness if they only look at you. Yes, the treasure is in a jar of clay. Why? To prevent others from confusing My incomparable power with your faithful service.

You remember that most of the time. You will be surrounded and battered by tough times—but not crushed; not sure of what to do at times—but not in despair; spiritually terrorized—but aware that I have not left your side; struck down—but not destroyed. Consider what Jesus endured and know some of it will come your way, too. But the life of Jesus will also be revealed in you. As a servant of My kingdom your life is sacrificed so that the life of Jesus may be revealed in your mortal body. Such service will help the blind see as Jesus lives in and through you.

Servanthood involves assisting other human beings on The Journey. Servanthood becomes an expression of your gratitude for My work in your life and an act of submission to My authority. Everyone needs help—and all the more in these times. These are difficult times and they will continue to be until the day of Jesus' return. Consider how people are self-absorbed, money hungry, self-promoting, proud, abusive, disobedient, contemptuous of their parents, ungrateful, unholy, it's dog-eat-dog, loveless relationships, unforgiving, slanderous, impulsively wild, lacking self-control, brutal, not lovers of good, cynical, treacherous, ruthless, conceited, lovers of pleasure rather than lovers of Me; some make a show of religion with a form of godliness but deny its power.

There are some who are always learning but never able to acknowledge the truth. They follow promoters of religious fads, exploited followers. I called Paul out of darkness and Timothy was his apprentice. Paul served Timothy with his life, teaching, and journey. To live for Me leads to some level of persecution, especially as the spiritual deterioration continues leading to the end of this age.

So what do you need? What are you to do? Be an obedient servant in your world.

How do you live there? Build your life on the Holy Scriptures;

stick with the truth. My Word shows you the way to salvation through faith in Christ Jesus, My Son. I gave life to every part of Scripture; it is useful in servanthood for:

1. Teaching—showing the Truth

2. Rebuking—exposing rebellion

3. Correcting—making mistakes right

4. Training in righteousness—revealing how to live life My way.

Yes, My Word puts you back together and equips you for My assignments.

Servanthood means you follow Jesus' example.

Servanthood is about helping others with life.

Servanthood is about the life of Jesus being manifest in your ordinary life.

Servanthood moves your focus off self onto others.

Servanthood is for fellow believers and those searching for the Answer.

Servanthood means you live the life.

Servanthood can be a simple act of kindness or a cup of cool water offered in My name.

Servanthood is at some level about every person you meet.

Jesus washed the feet of His disciples on the way to the cross ... imagine.

I love you,
Abba

YOUR HEART

In your quiet time with God, ask Him this question: "Father, what would You like to say to me today?" Write what you believe He is saying to you. Write your name, and begin to capture whatever

comes to mind, just as if God were speaking to you. For you see, He is ...

Now, take a moment to write your thoughts to our Father.

Here are a few questions to help you as you reflect on servanthood:

- Who has come alongside you on your journey? How did they serve you? What was the impact on your life?

- How well do you live in the moment?

- What impact does living in the now have on servanthood?

Prayer

Father, grace me to be obedient to Your call on my life. To serve as I step into the troubled lives of people who need a hand. Fill me with Your joy and peace, the power of Your Holy Spirit, so my life spills over with hope—not just for myself, but anyone I meet. Be exalted. In the name of our Savior and Lord, Jesus, amen

Week 48

THE CALL OF JESUS

Devotional Scriptures

Luke 7:36–50
Mark 5:1–20
Matthew 9:1–12
Acts 9:10–18
Luke 6:27–36
John 9:1–41

The Psalmist's Pen

Psalm 139

FROM STEVE'S HEART

When I tell people I grew up in Neodesha, few have heard of it and even fewer have any idea where my hometown is located. Most often they respond, "Oh, I know where Neosho, Missouri is!" Well Neodesha is located in Southeast Kansas and was settled by the Osage Indians in the early 1800's.

The name Neodesha comes from the Osage word for "where waters meet." My hometown is situated between the Verdigris River and Fall River. Yes, floods have been a challenge, especially those so called "100 year floods."

I remain thankful for my small town upbringing, but the chief blessing of my life is the Christian heritage given me by both sides of my family. A favorite picture of mine is this black and white photograph of my dad holding me when I was a toddler. Beyond the proof of how cute I was is the hand-written inscription on the back. Written in pencil with her large handwriting my great grandmother wrote...

> James Laswell and there (sic) Darling little Baby Boy.
> May the good Lord reward him for His work sake.
> Grandma Norman–with love–

Whether this "prayer of blessing" was for my Dad or for me I'm not sure; but it means a lot to me. And today, I want to agree, "May the good Lord reward him for His work sake."

My life journey began September 4, 1954 in the Wilson County Hospital. My spiritual birth is traced back to the Neodesha Church of the Nazarene. It was common back then for local churches to have regular "revival meetings."

When I was a first or second grader, Rev. Johnny Whistler, a traveling evangelist came to Neodesha for such an occasion. There are several things that stand out in my memory about that particular week:

1. Rev. Whistler was blind, but he sang, played the piano, and preached every night starting on Sunday

2. As part of the offering we brought cans of dog food for his seeing eye dog

3. It was during his preaching that I first responded to the Gospel; I heard the call of Jesus to follow Him and accepted Him as my personal Savior

As you know that was only the beginning. Growing up in the church and a Christian home I began to understand my Savior's call was not a onetime prayer for the forgiveness of my sins. The call of Jesus comes daily with The Journey.

Over time, I began to recognize the call of Jesus also was about more than the forgiveness of my sins. His call was for all my heart, soul, mind, body, and spirit … the total commitment of my life to His Lordship and Kingdom purposes.

The seasons of life and changing roles along The Journey presents me the opportunity to hear Jesus' call to deny myself and follow Him. Our willingness to die to self-rule allows me to embrace the life and freedom that only comes when we are led by His Holy Spirit. Although simple, it is not a quick fix. Although a faith transaction, it requires a lifetime to live out. The Journey is about answering the call of Jesus today and tomorrow until today is no more.

Do you remember when you first heard the *Savior* Jesus Christ call you by name?

Have you heard the *Lord* Jesus Christ call your name?

How have your responded? How will you respond?

Here is what I received: simply ask our Father, *"What would you like to say to me today?"*

FROM THE FATHER'S HEART

I know you. You're an open book before Me; I always have you in My sight. Yes, I am everywhere: behind you, beside you, and ahead of you. What I want you to understand is this: I am here to reassure you every step of the way—coming or going—I know you, call you by name, and believe in you.

There is no place you'll ever find yourself that I'm not there—high or low, east or west—even the darkness is not dark to Me. It's all the same to Me. Can you own this? I know you and believe in you.

And oh, yes, I shaped you, formed you in the secret place of your mother's womb. You are marvelously made—inside and out, body and soul, bit by bit—your life stages are spread out before Me. The days of your life, all prepared before you even lived one day of them. *Rest in that.*

Look, My thoughts are beyond your ability to comprehend in full—too vast to capture and box up. So get up each morning and live within this truth; live in My presence and calling of your name, your heart, soul, mind, and body as a living sacrifice. The day will come when wickedness will be done away with for good, but not just yet. Until that day there will be those who hate Me, as already demonstrated by man's response to Jesus. Self-inflated, godless arrogance is all a part of the human condition.

Having answered the call of Jesus on your life, I will investigate your life and provide you a clear picture of what you are to be about. You may count on Me to guide you on the road to eternal life. Such is My faithfulness, love, mercy, and grace for *all* who believe and answer the call. Take heart. Live well in My peace.

You must be on guard as one who has answered the call of Jesus. Here's what will happen if you begin to think your need of forgiveness is less than that of another person—your love and gratitude will be minimized.

The call of Jesus is hard to hear by those with no need. Consider the town harlot. Everyone in the village knew her business—some self-righteously judged and condemned her, others wanted her services, and others did not see her life as having value.

Yet she heard about Jesus and not just about Him, she heard the call of His heart on her life of misery and shame. Weeping, she washed His feet—wiped them with her hair, kissed, and anointed them with her very expensive perfume. Yes, she acted foolishly in front of the Pharisee and his guests that evening; and to think, she wasn't even an invited guest! Can you imagine the obstacles, the social pressure, her self-talk, and all those voices telling her *not* to enter his home saying "you'll make a fool of yourself…what will those men think…what will Jesus think?"

But she answered the call of Jesus on her broken heart and pain-filled life. Her weeping produced so many tears she washed the feet of Jesus with them. Out of her brokenness she accepted His call. She lost herself in the moment of encountering Jesus.

Yes, she was guilty of many sins. She understood that better than anyone else at the table, hence the magnitude of her love and gratitude. If forgiveness is perceived to be minimal, the expression of gratitude and love expressed will be minimal, too.

My invitation to sinners is a call of love and forgiveness; that evening the town harlot—the guest of the Guest went home a new person. She loved much knowing she was forgiven much.

How difficult is it for the town harlot around you? Have you been forgiven little? Or will you join her at the feet of Jesus weeping with deep gratitude and passionate love?

The call of Jesus is not just to the woman of the village—the town harlot; it is for you as one forgiven much. Come and worship demonstrate a spirit of gratitude; love with all your heart, soul, mind, body and strength as you remember My grace. Do not hinder My grace in your life or the broken and hurting lost around you...

I love you,
Abba

YOUR HEART

In your quiet time with God, ask Him this question: "Father, what would You like to say to me today?" Write what you believe He is saying to you. Write your name, and begin to capture whatever comes to mind, just as if God were speaking to you. For you see, He is...

Now, take a moment to write your thoughts to our Father.

Here are a few questions and suggestions to help you as you reflect upon the call of Jesus:

- How does the reality of God being with you, all the time impact your life today?

- If God shaped you, how might that impact how you feel about you? How do you want it to impact your thoughts about yourself?

- "If forgiveness is perceived to be minimal, the expression of

gratitude and love expressed will be minimal, too." What are your thoughts on God's forgiveness in your life?

Prayer

Father, forgive me for my failure to worship at the feet of Jesus my Savior and Lord as one who has been forgiven much. Have mercy upon me, lest I forget. I receive Your grace to live in the freedom of the forgiven ... humble before You, resisting the temptation of self-righteousness and a judgmental spirit. May those who are hurting and broken in my world see me as one who has been forgiven much and thus, loving You much. In the compassionate and loving name of Jesus, amen

Week 49

HUMANITY

Devotional Scriptures

Romans 8:1–17
2 Timothy 1:1–14
1 Peter 2:21–25
Romans 14:1–21
Matthew 6:25–34
Matthew 19:16–29

The Psalmist's Pen

Psalm 4

FROM STEVE'S HEART

What is and what is yet to be.

That seems to sum up The Journey as a human being … what is and what is yet to be. Our lives consistent with reality while at the same time being shaped according to the new reality available only through a restored relationship with God.

Yes, we are members of this special group of God's creation called humanity. We exhibit the form, nature, and qualities of such; likewise, we manifest the frailties and weaknesses associated with membership in this imperfect company. At the same time, we have a renewed relationship with God. We have received His gift of spiritual life allowing us to overcome the limitations of our weakened state. The Journey is about becoming genuine and enjoying accurate realignment with God's original design for us.

True humanity—everyone has experienced both aspects—is a matter of degree. Thankfully, my life has not been a demonstration of the worst of true humanity; still, there I go, but for the grace of God! Only by His grace do I desire the transformation of my true fallen humanity into my true Christ like humanity. By His mercy, we overcome the frailties and weaknesses common to our lot while alive on this planet. To love, forgive, submit and serve…genuine, consistent with being a follower of Jesus. True humanity—this incredible treasure in jars of clay, the life of Jesus—manifests in our mortal bodies.

It seems this season of transition with significant testing and hard times is not exactly what I signed up for. The reality of my true humanity is being made evident. Yes, I fight admitting it. Who wants to struggle in the face of opposition? I don't want to grieve the loss; still, heartfelt grief seeks me out, uninvited. I don't want to doubt whether I'm on the right path today or not; still, questions attack my mind, uninvited. I don't want to see my loved ones in pain, wrestling with their journey; still, the details bring some heartache, for now. "What is, and is yet to be…" that is plight of true humanity.

The Journey is our common denominator. Human beings living by faith (or not…) in the One Perfect Human—the Son of Man, the Son of God, Jesus Christ our Lord and Savior! Come Jesus, live in me, take all of me, and transform me into true humanity.

Here is what I received; simply ask Abba, *"What would You like to say to me today?"*

FROM THE FATHER'S HEART

I declare you righteous in Christ in response to your faith.

I have always cared for you; even now, as you call out to Me. I hear your cry for help and will have mercy upon you. How sad that humanity turns My glory into shame. How? By the worship of illusions and acceptance of lies from little-g-gods; they can do nothing to help you.

Be assured and mark this well: I have set the redeemed apart for Myself...I choose you. Call to Me; I will listen the very moment you cry out to Me.

As part of humanity, you are prone to complain to speak out in anger lashing out at Me. It's not that I can't handle it. Stand in awe before Me, I am God, and you are not. Be still and know that I am God; lie quietly before Me meditating on this. Place your trust in Me and present yourself a pleasing sacrifice.

People constantly want more without giving thought to My gifts already given. Some chide, "Who can show us any good? God is not helping." Let the light of My face shine upon you; let this be enough—My joy. My joy lasts and is greater than their fleeting celebrations of victory. Find rest in Me as I put your life back together.

True humanity acknowledges Me as the one true God—faithful, listening, compassionate, and worthy of your worship. You know this. Don't let others pull you back into foolish pursuits and false reality.

The Journey calls you to be real. You are a human being—not simplistic, but complex and created in Our image; not perfect but characterized by the frailties and weaknesses associated with being an imperfect human being. You are human not divine. The more you accept and understand, the better your life experience—less baggage. You will be free of pretense and hypocrisy while allowing others and yourself to be reshaped as originally created.

Along The Journey, as you wait for all things to be made right and grow weary, this is My promise: My Holy Spirit will help you in your weakness. So when you don't know how to pray will you purpose to cooperate with Me? My Spirit will pray in and for you even making prayer out of your wordless sighs and groaning. Look, even now He keeps you present before Me; and He knows you better than you know yourself. He will get you through. So be confident, every detail in your life, My child, is being worked into something good.

From the beginning, I determined to shape your life—the lives of all who love Me—along the same lines as Jesus' life. Your life is being conformed to the likeness of My Son; He stands first in the long line of true humanity restored.

True humanity is revealed in Jesus—the original and intended pattern for your life. Once I made the decision what My children would be like, I called each by name. Having answered My call, you have been set right with Me. Having been set right with Me through the righteousness of Jesus, I am committed to stay with you to the very end, gloriously completing what I began.

Consider this: I put everything on the line for you. I embraced your condition and exposed Myself to the worst humanity could do when I sent My own Son. Do you think there is anything else I wouldn't gladly do for you? Really?

Jesus died and was raised to life for you! He is here at this very moment sticking up for you. Do you think anyone or anything can drive a wedge between Our love and you? Trouble? Hard times? Hatred? Hunger? Homelessness? Bullying threats? Backstabbing? Don't let this opposition faze you—We love you. Nothing living or dead, angelic or demonic, today or tomorrow, high or low, thinkable or unthinkable—absolutely nothing—can come between you and My love for you. This is because of the way Jesus, your Master and Savior, embraces you.

Since I am on your side like this, how can you lose? I've put it all on the line—will you work with Me? Come up to the balcony and see. Step out of the busy madness you call living. Be still and recognize Me, understand this: I am God … above everything. I will be exalted. Say it, knowing it is true: "The Lord Almighty is with us, the God of Jacob is our tower and stronghold, our fortress."

Every detail of your life, as one who loves Me and is called by My name, is being worked into something good. Look at the big picture. This means transformation of your true humanity into the likeness of Jesus—true humanity.

I love you,
Abba

YOUR HEART

In your quiet time with God, ask Him this question: "Father, what would You like to say to me today?" Write what you believe He is saying to you. Write your name, and begin to capture whatever comes to mind, just as if God were speaking to you. For you see, He is ...

Now, take a moment to write your thoughts to our Father.

Here are a few questions to help you as you reflect upon being a part of humanity:

- How does the idea of Jesus choosing you make you feel?

- What area of weaknesses do you need the Holy Spirit's help with today?

- Where in your life do you want to work with God more closely? What is the desired outcome?

Prayer

Father, thank You for calling me by name and calling me to Yourself. Thank You for not leaving me, as You found me in my true humanity but hold out the promise and path to be transformed into the likeness of Jesus ... my true humanity. By Your grace I will not give up. It is my ambition to be pleasing to You every day, today. Today, empower me by Your Holy Spirit to live my human experience authentically, as one raised from the dead, victorious in the victory of Jesus! In the name of the Son of Man and Son of God, Jesus, amen

Week 50
FAITHFUL WITNESS

Devotional Scriptures

Philippians 1:12–18
Luke 12:1–12
Colossians 4:1–6
Matthew 20:1–16
John 5:30–47
Acts 10:34–38

The Psalmist's Pen

Psalm 16

FROM STEVE'S HEART

Recently I did a simple exercise designed to identity my values. The seemingly simple assignment was to review a list of twenty values and select my top five. Easy enough, right? The instructions were easy; the exercise itself can be more difficult. You see, to select five values means I had to declare and release fifteen lesser-in-value values.

Next I was to review those top five values to determine the integrity of my life. How do you know what you value? How do you determine if there is conflict between your values? Consider a conversation and cross-examination of the faithful witness. And who is this faithful witness? My life and yours—the calendar, behavior, choices, priorities, and actions—they all stand firm, worthy of trust, consistently revealing the truth of the matter; the evidence speaks.

It worked. There was one value that is important to me, family, but it did not make the cut; it was crowded out of the top five. Yes, it was a bit shocking to me. Yes, it was pretty easy to explain how I got here. Yes, it was a wakeup call. The exercise accomplished its objective revealing to me the truth about my life. It was time for a tweak, so my life and core values were aligned; something would need to change.

Jesus is the Faithful Witness. He is worthy of our trust and belief regarding God and life. The Bible makes it clear He revealed all that we need to know to live now and be prepared for life after death.

The Journey calls us to be a faithful witness as followers of Jesus. The Journey often presents us an exercise or reality check. So we participate in the means of grace (those ways of growing as a believer and staying connected in our faith … Baptism, the Lord's Supper, Worship, Bible Study and prayer, Personal Quiet Time, meditation and reflection). Our lives, by God's grace, are empowered so we live a life consistent with this faith-fact: Jesus is our Savior and Lord—we are forgiven, so we forgive. We are loved, so we love. We have hope, so we wait in expectation. We have peace, so we don't worry. We have joy, so we have strength for today.

Still, Jesus is the Faithful Witness. *Our lives and our words must always point people to Jesus for only then are we a Faithful Witness.*

Here is what I received. Ask our Father, "*What would You like to say to me today?*"

FROM THE FATHER'S HEART

Whatever your lot in life, whatever you're going through, remain conscious of the effect your response has on the Message. You see, your life as a follower of Jesus has an influence on how the Gospel impacts the lives of others.

For example, consider Paul. He was in prison because of his devotion and loyalty to Christ. He consistently reported what he knew to be true: the life, death, burial, and resurrection of Jesus Christ, the Messiah.

Yes, his life demonstrates that of a faithful witness. Early on he sought to destroy the church going house to house, dragging followers of Jesus, men and women off to prison. Then he encountered Jesus. From his faith-encounter and transformation he was imprisoned. Why? His consistent truth-telling message about Jesus; Paul was firmly and devotedly supportive of the Gospel and his life message gave evidence.

To be a faithful witness your focus must remain on Jesus. How grieved I am with organized religion; how easy for you to become faithful to your agenda. Don't get caught up in judging the motives of others when it comes to the preaching of the Gospel. What matters is that Jesus Christ is proclaimed as Savior.

Do you think we could adjust your perspective a bit? As a faithful witness, look at everything that happens in your journey from My viewpoint and ask yourself: "Am I being a credible follower of Jesus providing evidence of His rule in my life? Does my life point others to Jesus?" Faithful witnesses live with the conviction and desire to make Jesus real—no matter what!

Live in such a way that your life gives a credit to the Gospel. It's all about people putting their trust in Christ. In order for this to happen, be My faithful witness—point people to Jesus. You have experienced the impact of the Message now give evidence with your response to life. How? Stand firm, united with other believers, contending as one for the Gospel helping others place their trust in Christ. There is more to life than trusting in Christ for there is suffering as well. Both are a part of your relationship with Me in Christ. So don't be frightened in anyway by such opposition.

A faithful witness lives in a manner worthy of the Gospel of Christ; then you will consistently and constantly point to Jesus, The Faithful Witness.

I love you,
Abba

YOUR HEART

In your quiet time with God, ask Him this question: "Father, what would You like to say to me today?" Write what you believe He is saying to you. Write your name, and begin to capture whatever comes to mind, just as if God were speaking to you. For you see, He is . . .

Now, take a moment to write your thoughts to our Father.

Here are a couple of questions to help you as you reflect upon Jesus, as the faithful witness:

- How would you evaluate your witness as a follower of Jesus?

- What would make your witness more powerful?

Prayer

Father, thank You for Your Son's faithful witness. How He reveals You, Your wisdom, Your heart for us, and Your redemptive plan of salvation. Help me be a faithful witness by using my life and words to point others to Your Son, Jesus, our Savior. Grant me grace to live a consistent life as Your child bringing glory and honor to You. In Jesus' name, amen

Week 51

TRANSFORMING POWER

Devotional Scriptures

2 Corinthians 3:4–18
1 Peter 1:3–2:3
Hebrews 1:1–4
Jeremiah 32:16–27
Luke 9:1–6
Luke 24:36–53

The Psalmist's Pen

Psalm 66

FROM STEVE'S HEART

The classroom was filled with excitement and enthusiasm on that Friday morning in May. The seniors were in that bittersweet twilight zone of high school graduation. They had arrived, but talked about beginning again and in the real world. The same conversations and words will be repeated again this spring. But one faculty member always seemed to take more interest in her students than just the subject matter at hand. As they celebrated their accomplishments, she gave a writing assignment, a final exam.

The simple instructions were seemingly inappropriate for such a glorious moment along the journey: *"Write your life story thirty years down the road; include how your decisions will impact your future.*

In particular, include those that lead you to experience some measure of failure or difficult times or consequences." That was the assignment; write their story thirty years down the road and not just how successful they were going to be.

Truth is, not one of them was able to write their story accurately. As someone has said, "Truth is stranger than fiction." If given a legal pad and pen, which of us having experienced life's successes and failures could have written our stories?

This past week I had lunch with a brother who brought greetings and a brief update on an individual who had worked for me. The story is sad, almost tragic, filled with pain and unfortunate consequences including a broken marriage, health issues, children struggling in school, stressed-out with court proceedings, job changes, and weariness. No question, she would never have completed her senior writing assignment twenty years ago with the story that is now her life story. Still her life, her story, is not out of the reach of God's transforming power.

The tone of our conversation was not marked by judgment or condemnation but compassion. For we acknowledged, "There go I but for the grace of God." Then, my friend shared how grateful he is to God for his wife, marriage, and family; you see his marriage was nearly destroyed a few years ago. Yes, another story of God's transforming power at work in human lives.

So as a high school senior, what would you have written? And today, how have you experienced God's transforming power? Where in your life do you need God to release His transforming power today?

Here is what I received. Will you ask our Father, *"What would You like to say to me today?"*

FROM THE FATHER'S HEART

Transformation is My gift of a restored personal relationship, a purpose-lived life, and eternity together. All this is made possible because Jesus was resurrected from the dead. Don't be alarmed, I am keeping watch over history; the day of total transformation when your life will be healed and whole is coming.

Yes this is good news of great joy when you are thinking clearly, even in the midst of all kinds of aggravation, grief, and trials. As a reminder, your faith is proved genuine when it comes through the refining fire of The Journey that includes a measure of suffering. When Jesus returns, to wrap all this up, it will be your faith that I will display as evidence of His victory.

Your total salvation is coming because of your faith. You have never seen Jesus, but you love Him. In fact, you still don't see Him, yet you trust in Him with inexpressible and glorious joy. Why? You are already receiving the goal of your faith—a transformed life; you are raised from the spiritually dead and alive in Christ. You are there now—rejoice!

Prophets of old told of this age asked a lot of questions about My promise, the Messiah. They wanted to know who and when. You know the answer. Think about it. The pivotal event of salvation history occurred before your birth; the message of Israel's prophets fulfilled—angels even long to look into this. Do you realize how fortunate you are?

My transforming power is fully available at this time in history. Prepare your mind to engage in clear thinking, live with self-control; set your hope only on My grace that will be fully revealed when Jesus returns. This means live according to the pattern of Jesus' life as My obedient child. Cooperate with Me, so your life shape follows the way of life modeled by Jesus: energetic, holy, and set apart for Me. Don't slip back into the old way of life—selfish, self-centered, self-governed, self-destructive, and doing whatever you like. Live worthy of the call that comes from Me through Jesus: total surrender.

A couple of thoughts to help you live here and now as My person:

Call out for help; I am committed to you; don't grow weary

Remember this world is not your final home...

Travel The Journey cultivating a consciousness of My presence

Remember the cost of your transformation—the sacred blood of My Son, Jesus Christ

It's all tied to His death and resurrection your hope for the future

Transformation is about change, restoring you to life—the nature, function, condition, and future of your life. When you obeyed the truth you purified yourself as demonstrated by how you love others. Support your decision to live committed and unselfish in all your relationships. Love, is to want what is best for others regardless of their response. Love as I love you. This is your new way of life. Your original birth came from mortal sperm; your new birth is the result your faith in My living Word. This is the Gospel you have been taught.

Transformation is about change leading you to maturity. My word has the ability and capacity to change you from a selfish, rebellious, disobedient, dead-in-sin human being to a follower and imitator of Jesus—pure, loving, and obedient. That's what I make available to you.

I love you,
Abba

YOUR HEART

In your quiet time with God, ask Him this question: "Father, what would You like to say to me today?" Write what you believe He is saying to you. Write your name, and begin to capture whatever comes to mind, just as if God were speaking to you. For you see, He is...

Now, take a moment to write your thoughts to our Father.

Here are a couple of questions to help you reflect on God's transforming power:

- God is watching over history; how will this truth impact your life today?

- What advantage does your time in history—centuries after Jesus' birth, death, and resurrection—have on your outlook today? How do you want it to?

- In what ways have you already experienced the transforming, changing power of God in your life? Perhaps you want to express your appreciation to Abba at this time...

Prayer

Heavenly Father, I cannot imagine where my life would be today if not for Your transforming power! Thank You! It is my desire to live in total surrender to the Lordship of Jesus. My desire is to cooperate with You and Your ability to change my heart and life, so I live free of sin's dominion and for Your glory. It is my desire to receive Your grace so deeply that Jesus lives in me today—through my life, just as I am. Taking my talents, personality, history, skills, life experience, ambition, potential, and humanity—all set apart for Your glory. Jesus' life lived through my mortal being, Your transforming power revealed... my life, a witness to those still searching for the Answer, pointing to Jesus—the Way, the Truth, and the Life. Help.... In the name of our Servant Lord and Savior, Jesus, amen.

Week 52

THE KING

Devotional Scriptures

Matthew 16:21–28
John 6:15–21
John 1:43–51
Acts 17:1–9
1 Corinthians 15:20–28
Revelation 1:1–8

The Psalmist's Pen

Psalm 47

FROM STEVE'S HEART

I'm not a movie buff by any stretch, but Rita and I occasionally enjoy those epic films that offer a view of history and the lives of royalty. Often, part of the enjoyment is the language. The way they speak encourages good listening just so I can understand what is said. Sometimes it is the pageantry.

Occasionally there will be a phrase that strikes me and I pick up on it for a while. Such was the case with the phrase "my lady" as in: "As you wish, my lady." So, for a few days I responded to Rita, "As you wish, my Lady." Yes, that's about as close to living the life of royalty, pomp, and pageantry as we'll ever know.

This past week I found myself singing the words of the hymn, "King of My Life I Crown Thee Now"...

> *King of my life, I crown Thee now,*
> *Thine shall the glory be;*
> *Lest I forget Thy thorn crowned brow,*
> *Lead me to Calvary.*

> *Refrain:*
> *Lest I forget Gethsemane,*
> *Lest I forget Thine agony;*
> *Lest I forget Thy love for me,*
> *Lead me to Calvary.*

> *May I be willing, Lord, to bear*
> *Daily my cross for Thee;*
> *Even Thy cup of grief to share,*
> *Thou hast borne all for me.*

> *Refrain:*
> *Lest I forget Gethsemane,*
> *Lest I forget Thine agony;*
> *Lest I forget Thy love for me,*
> *Lead me to Calvary.*

Sometimes it is easy to forget what Scripture says about Jesus, the King of kings. Sometimes I can forget He is The King and I am His servant; bond-servant... free to go but compelled by His love, I make the choice to stay.

Jesus, born of the Virgin Mary, the Son of God and Son of Man, the Messiah, Savior, Master, and Teacher. The crucified Jesus crowned with a crown of thorns on the cross where the charge against Him was posted: "This is Jesus, the King of the Jews." (Matthew 27:37) Indeed, lead me to Calvary.

One of the criminals who hung beside Him recognized Him

and said, "Jesus, remember me when You come into Your kingdom." (Luke 23:42) Today, I am reminded that King Jesus told that dying thief "... today you will be with Me in paradise." (Luke 23:43) Once again I crown Thee, King of my life.

Today, I remind myself of His words "My kingdom is not of this world" (John 18:36); especially when it seems those who dishonor my King are getting away with it.

Today, I take heart believing that one day every knee will bow and every tongue will confess that Jesus Christ is the Lord, the King.

By definition, a king rules for life.

By *invitation*, King Jesus rules in my heart! Hallelujah!

Here is what I received. Ask our Father, "*What would You like to say to me today?*"

FROM THE FATHER'S HEART

In their enthusiasm over the miracle of free food, the crowd wanted to make Jesus king by their own doing. He slipped away to be alone in the hills—not just to get away, but to remain connected to Me. Sometimes people want to make Jesus King on their terms. A king you can make is of little good. That's not how it is with Christ the King; you can't control Him for your own purpose. It is your commitment to Jesus that brings you into alignment with Me.

The disciples needed to get to Capernaum; daylight was fading. They were three to four miles out on the lake when a storm blew in. Not fun for them. Through the storm Jesus came to them. They were frightened by this Jesus' unusual appearance; He had to assure them it was okay before they wanted Him on board. During the storm, are you willing to take Jesus on board? Sure enough, with Jesus on board, the disciples arrived exactly where they were headed.

My desire for you is that you ...
see Jesus for who He is ... the Messiah

trust Jesus for what He does … deliver you from sin
align yourself with Jesus … enter into real life, eternal life.

Jesus was sent to put you back on your feet alive and whole. Every detail I assigned Him will be completed. His birth, death, and resurrection were executed perfectly. The only historical event remaining is His return for all who embrace Christ the King. Time, as you know it will be over—you will enter eternity with My gift of eternal life.

Jesus saw Nathanael under the fig tree. For the people of his day to be found sitting under the fig tree indicated a person was at peace. Is that why you come here to this table, this place, your personal quiet time with Me? Do you come seeking peace? Do you come to learn of My ways so you may walk in My paths? Do you come to Me longing for peace on earth, good will toward men as promised with the gift of Jesus?

Nathanael was sitting under his fig tree longing for the promised Messiah, the King of Israel. Jesus not only saw him sitting under a fig tree. He saw deep into his heart. The longings of his heart, his dreams, and his prayers—that was what lead Jesus to pay tribute, "Here is a true Israelite, in whom there is nothing false."

Nathanael, a student of the prophets, was an authentic seeker of truth. Now he was given the opportunity to declare the identity of this one from Nazareth: "Rabbi, you are the Son of God; you are the King of Israel."

Take heart as you seek peace in this place of quiet. You believe My Message. Jesus is the victorious King of kings and Lord of lords. Let your peace, in the midst of The Journey be undisturbed knowing Christ the King is King and is coming again.

Worship Him; give glory and power to Christ, who loves you. Worship this One who frees you from your sins, by His own blood and made you to be a kingdom and priest to serve Me.

Worship Him—the loyal witness, the firstborn from the dead, Ruler over all earthly kings.

Worship Christ the King. He is coming again and will be seen by every eye, those who mocked and killed Him will see Him; people from all nations and all times will mourn because of Him. So shall it be. He is the A to Z; the God Who is, the God Who was, and the God about to arrive, the Almighty, Sovereign-strong, King Jesus!

Let your heart response to life be shaped by your response to Christ the King. Do not let the hard times, the hostility of the world, or the opposition of Satan detour you. Do not allow your disappointments or trials to hinder your worship of Christ the King! Don't let go of My peace, My vision, or your hope built on Christ the King!

I love you,
Abba

Note:

Perhaps to assist your worship of Christ the King, listen to Handel's "Messiah Hallelujah Chorus."

YOUR HEART

In your quiet time with God, ask Him this question: "Father, what would You like to say to me today?" Write what you believe He is saying to you. Write your name, and begin to capture whatever comes to mind, just as if God were speaking to you. For you see, He is …

Now, take a moment to write your thoughts to our Father.

Here are a couple of questions to help you reflect on Christ the King:

- How have you tried to make God the way you wanted Him to be?

- How receptive or connected are you to Jesus during a storm in your life?

- What is your typical response to God when hurting, afraid, or confused?

- How does recognizing Christ the King help you navigate your journey?

Prayer

Our Father, Glory to Christ the King! What grace to know and confess Jesus as my Master, Savior, and Lord; the Messiah, the King! Amazing grace! What grace to trust in You, God Almighty—Father, Son, and Holy Spirit—to rest in Your peace, to draw strength from Your joy, to have confidence from placing all my hope in You... Hallelujah! You are God, and I am not... only to be a willing servant of Christ the King. In the name of Christ the King, amen

Week 53

FRESH START

Devotional Scriptures

Proverbs 29:18
2 Timothy 3:10–17
Ephesians 3:14–20

The Psalmist's Pen

Psalm 21

FROM STEVE'S HEART

Do you appreciate the way God has designed life with fresh starts?
I certainly do.

It can be as simple as a new minute. Think about it. During
the next sixty seconds you can choose to forgive an offense or let
it ago ... again. Yes, God's grace in this moment offers you a fresh
start as you receive forgiveness and "forgive those who transgress
against us." But that is just one example; God's Fresh Start covers
all of life.

This minute you can choose to think differently, to believe, to
change your expectations, to do the right thing.

This minute you can make a choice that will move you toward
your destiny, toward greater intimacy with God.

This minute holds a fresh start.

Of course we measure time with hours, days, weeks, months,

years, decades, and centuries too; every metric offers a fresh start. God's fresh start is available as often as needed. Think about it. The rising of the sun signals the opportunity to begin again. The seven days have a Sunday for both rest and God's call on our lives to "Come, begin again your pursuit of knowing, loving, and serving Me." Motivated by love, God continually offers us opportunities for renewal and restoration—moments to begin again, time to step into life with renewed vigor on The Journey!

So have you scheduled your appointment to reflect on your past twelve months? It's part of my transition-tradition between calendar years. I review my journal for lessons learned, high points, challenges, and life lessons. May I encourage you to rehearse your life: feedback, experience, successes, and failures? To remember God's faithfulness—how He turned worries that appeared so big but never happened, how Abba resolved them. Yes, I know we still wait for answers. Will you let your heart take courage as you wait in expectation for His answer?

Your end-of-year review allows the Holy Spirit to prepare your heart and mind for today and the yet to be written next chapter of The Journey. This is a big fresh start, so seize the moment.

As you reflect, notice the gifts and blessings and be appreciative. Rehearse how God has demonstrated His love, faithfulness, mercy, and grace. Perhaps that will turn into a time of praise and you will find yourself bowing in worship before our Father, the Lord God Almighty.

Bring your thanksgiving offering and lift your praise, bow in adoration as your worship moves into confession. Yes, it is appropriate for your appointment to include confession—the confessing of your faith and your sins. Yes we know that if we confess our sins God is faithful and just to forgive our sins and to cleanse us from all unrighteousness.

Now, I have a question for you, perhaps to answer during your transition quiet time. Your answers may come easy or you may have to work at it. Your answers have power. The question is simple: "What are your dreams?"

Take a notebook or your journal and set aside some time today, tomorrow, and the next day to start listing your dreams. Your dream list could include areas such as physical, emotional, intellectual, spiritual, material, professional, financial, creative, adventure, legacy, mental, and character. It's your dream list penciled in, in the presence of the Dream Giver.

What are your dreams? Start writing—don't critique them; just capture them. It's an exercise. Once you capture your thoughts you will want to put together a plan to fulfill them.

Ask God to guide you

Tell someone, a friend about your list

Ask about their list

Find someone to hold you accountable to your plan, to the next step

Find your cheerleaders, the people who are a part of your support system

Now watch what happens. Let God bless this exercise and make it a part of your fresh start. Allow God's grace to renew your *energy for life,* for the next chapter. Some of your dreams could happen almost immediately, some in the next year, and others may be years in the making. Will you keep your dreams alive and in alignment with God's dreams for you?

Here is what I received. Ask our Father, *"What would You like to say to me today?"*

By the way, one of my dreams was to write a book. With this chapter, the hard part of writing The Journey is completed, one year later.

What's your dream?

FROM THE FATHER'S HEART

Where there is no dream … no vision people cast off restraint, they lose self-control, and self-discipline.

Ignorance, lack of knowledge, and not knowing Me leave you at a loss and lost on The Journey. When you can't see what I am doing, you will stumble and fall all over yourself; but when you listen to Me and pay attention to what I reveal you are blessed—set apart for Me. You will run wild if you ignore Me; how much better The Journey when you know, recognize, and keep My ways.

Redemptive revelations keep you from perishing, but if you want a life to be envied follow My ways. I have given and will give life to Scripture. The Bible is useful to show you the truth, expose your rebellion, correct your mistakes, and train you so know and keep My ways. My Word puts you together and shapes you for the tasks, the dreams, and the life I have for you today and for eternity.

So slow down and be responsive to Me, to My work in your life, and let's pursue the dream. Be captured by My vision for your life it will:

Protect you from reckless use of this limited resource—your brief life on earth

Guide you into the meaningful investment of this limited resource—your earthly life, and

Reward you with a purpose driven investment of this limited resource—your life.

As you pursue Me, the God of all Creation, I will strengthen you by My Holy Spirit. I will give you inner strength; I work from the inside out as you allow Christ to live in your heart. Stand firm in the reality of My love. Experience the extravagant dimensions: the amazing width and length, the incredible depth and height of My love for you. Know My love, not just about it, and receive power to live victoriously no matter what comes your way.

Remember, I can do anything!—far more than you can imagine, guess, or request in your wildest dreams. I am transforming you into the likeness of Christ. I can, I will, I am leading and guiding your steps. Let Me be your Shepherd.

Rejoice.

Glorify My Name.

Be glad in Jesus, My Son, and your Savior, the Messiah!

I love you … I really do love you,

Abba

YOUR HEART

In your quiet time with God, ask Him this question: "Father, what would You like to say to me today?" Write what you believe He is saying to you. Write your name, and begin to capture whatever comes to mind, just as if God were speaking to you. For you see, He is …

Now, take a moment to write your thoughts to our Father.

Here are a couple of questions to help you reflect on your fresh start:

- Is there an area of your life where you have cast off restraint? How would clarity regarding God's vision for your life help?

- How is the pace of life impacting your ability to slow down and be responsive to Abba?

- What is the significance of God as your Shepherd to you? How are you tapping into His leading?

Prayer

Abba, Thank You for the fresh starts. I need them in for my pursuit of knowing, loving, and serving You. Thank You for Your amazing grace, unconditional love, liberating mercy, and sustaining peace. Here am I; take me—all of me. I surrender to Your authority as God Almighty, to the Lordship of Jesus Christ, and to the invasion of Your Holy Spirit, my comforter and guide. Here am I; I am Yours, and You are mine. You are God, and I am not. In the name of Christ, the Author of my fresh start, amen

Footnote:

Two books have impacted me in this area of our dreams—*The Dream Giver* by Bruce Wilkinson and *The Dream Manager* by Matthew Kelly.

If you have interest in what is going on with Battle Plan for Believers or Steve Laswell's ministry please visit: www.battleplanforbelievers.com.

We have a faith-based anticipation and promise that God has only begun to release the ministry of *Battle Plan for Believers* to the Body of Christ. We watch and wait.

Thank you for joining *The Journey* … the community. I would love to hear from you.

Contact information is available on our website, as well.